THE One & Only cupcakes and muffins Cookbook

NEW HOLLAND

THE
One & Only
cupcakes
and muffins
Cookbook

All the recipes you will ever need

With a Foreword by
Jenny Linford

NEW
HOLLAND

First published by New Holland Publishers in 2012
London • Cape Town • Sydney • Auckland

www.newhollandpubishers.com

86 Edgware Road, London W2 2EA, United Kingdom

Wembley Square, Solan Road, Gardens, Cape Town 8001, South Africa

1/66 Gibbes Street, Chatswood, NSW 2067, Australia
www.newholland.com.au

218 Lake Road, Northcote, Auckland 0746, New Zealand

Created by
Pulp Media, Richmond, London

Project Editors: Emma Wildsmith and Helena Caldon
Art Director: Susi Martin
Illustrations: Kuo Kang Chen and Kate Simunek

Photography: Charlotte Tolhurst, Stockfood Ltd, Philip Wilkins: 60-61, 84-85, 128-129, 172-173, 194-195, Shutterstock.com: 1, 6, 10, 17, 18, 223, 224-5, 233, 238-239. Every effort has been made to credit photographers and copyright-holders. If any have been overlooked we will be pleased to make the necessary corrections in subsequent editions.

Publisher: James Tavendale
www.pulp.me.uk

A record of this book is available from the National Library.
ISBN 9781742572420
Printed in Italy
10 9 8 7 6 5 4 3 2 1

"You know life is good when
you have cupcakes in your hands
and a smile on your face."

anonymous

Contents

Foreword

By Jenny Linford

With home-baking very much in vogue these days, what could be nicer than conjuring up some freshly-baked delicious treats? American-style, sweet or savoury muffins (not to be confused with the plain, griddle-cooked 'English muffin') are increasingly popular as a breakfast snack. Dainty cupcakes, once the innocent preserve of children's tea parties, are now gloriously grown-up and fashionable. Much of their appeal is undoubtedly their versatility. They can be made in numerous forms and flavours, from classic vanilla or chocolate to sophisticated combinations such as quince and rose or rhubarb and elderflower. There is something very appealing about having the scent of baking cake filling your home and anticipation that comes with knowing you'll soon have a delicious treat to eat.

Be precise
Whereas most cookery allows for a degree of flexibility when it comes to quantities, baking really is an area where accuracy makes all the difference, enabling you to produce consistently good results. To that end, if you enjoy baking it's well worth buying a decent set of kitchen scales. There are many reasonably-priced models on the market which will be a great investment and last for many years. A set of measuring spoons are also very useful for measuring the correct amount of ingredients such as baking powder or vanilla extract.

Mixing properly
When making cupcakes, if creaming together the butter and sugar is required, do make sure to do this well. When folding in dry ingredients, however, do this lightly but thoroughly. Muffin mixtures require gentle handling. When it comes to folding the mixture together, take care not to over-mix or you'll lose the air and have heavy muffins as a result.

Filling correctly
Don't be over-generous when you're spooning your cupcake or muffin mixture into the cases. Only fill the cases two-thirds full to allow space for the mixture to rise. Muffins, especially, should rise out of their cases, creating a characteristic 'muffin-top' overhang.

Be prepared

As with any baking, preheating your oven beforehand to the required temperature is very important. Ovens vary hugely, so get to know yours and make adjustments accordingly. Once the cakes are in the oven, it's all too easy to get distracted and lose track of time. To prevent your cakes from burning, use a timer; it's a simple device which is so helpful when it comes to baking. Remember, however, that using a timer is just a prompt for you to check that a cake is cooked through rather than a sign that the cake is done. In baking, as with any cooking, common sense has a part to play. Test your cupcakes and muffins by inserting a fine skewer into one; if it comes out clean, then they are ready. If not, allow a few more minutes baking time and test again.

Visual appeal

An essential part of a cupcake's appeal is its pretty appearance. On the whole, cupcakes come with toppings, ranging from a smooth layer of glossy fondant icing to a generous dollop of luscious frosting. When it comes to making your toppings, one thing to remember is to use good-quality ingredients. Unsalted butter, for example, has a far better flavour and texture than a low-fat spread. Yes, it's indulgent, but that's the point of a cupcake – it's meant to be a treat. Similarly, if making a chocolate ganache to use as a topping, use good-quality dark chocolate as it will give a much better flavour and texture.

Cupcakes and Muffins

18

Make sure that you match the shape of your cupcake to your choice of topping. For an even base on which to spread your topping, simply carefully slice the domed top off your cupcake once it is cooled. These 'flat' cupcakes work well with smooth toppings such as royal icing. Domed cupcakes are good with thick, textured toppings such as cream cheese-based frosting.

Muffins, usually served free from any topping, have a more rustic appearance. In fact, a few imperfections such as cracks or burst berry stains are all part of their appeal. Seeing the ingredient with which a muffin is flavoured, whether it be classic blueberry or grated carrot, is attractive. For a finishing touch, you can sprinkle over an appropriate topping to the raw muffin mixture before baking to add flavour and texture – so crunchy Demerara sugar to a sweet muffin or grated cheese on a cheese one. On the whole, however, simplicity rules with muffins.

Cheese, bacon and sundried tomato muffins

1. Preheat the oven to 375°F (190°C). Line a muffin tray with 10 paper muffin cases.

2. In a large bowl, sift together the flour and baking powder.

3. Stir the sugar, salt, pepper, three-quarters of the cheese, bacon, sundried tomatoes and chives into the flour mixture and mix well.

4. In another bowl, whisk together the eggs, milk and melted butter. Pour this mixture over the dry ingredients. Stir until just mixed. The batter should remain slightly lumpy.

5. Fill the muffin cases, then sprinkle the tops with the reserved cheese.

6. Bake for 20–25 minutes until risen and firm. These can be served warm or cold.

Preparation time: 20 min
Cooking time: 25 min
Serves 10

275g plain flour
1 tbsp baking powder.
1 tsp caster sugar
1 tsp salt
½ tsp freshly ground black pepper
125g Cheddar cheese, grated
100g smoked back bacon rashers,
   grilled and chopped
75g sundried tomatoes, chopped
2 tbsp freshly snipped chives
2 eggs
200ml semi-skimmed milk
75g butter, melted

Banana and chocolate chip muffins

1. Preheat the oven to 400°F (200°C). Line a 12-hole muffin tray with paper cases, or just butter the tray.

2. In a large bowl, sift together the flour, baking powder and salt then stir in the sugar. In another bowl, mash the bananas with a fork. In a jug, whisk together the egg, milk and butter, then add to the mashed banana, stirring to combine.

3. Add this mixture to the flour mixture. Stir to mix, then fold in the chocolate chips.

4. Spoon into the prepared tin and bake for 20–25 minutes or until the tops are lightly browned and spring back when pressed gently. Served warm or cold.

Variation: if you prefer, use white chocolate chips or chunks.

Preparation time: 10 min
Cooking time: 25 min
Serves 12

275g plain flour
1 tbsp baking powder
½ tsp salt
125g caster sugar
2 large ripe bananas, peeled and
  roughly chopped
1 large egg
240ml milk
85g melted butter
175g milk and dark chocolate chips
  or chunks

Banoffee cupcakes

1. Line 2 x 12-hole cupcake trays with 16 paper cases. Preheat the oven to 350°F (180°C).

2. Whisk the butter or margarine and sugar with an electric whisk, until light and fluffy.

3. Gradually whisk in the eggs, with a little flour, then gently fold in the remaining flour, bananas and pecans.

4. Spoon the mixture evenly into the cupcake cases and level the tops. Bake in the oven for 15–20 minutes until they turn spongy and the tops are golden brown. Leave in the tin for a few minutes, then transfer to a wire rack.

5. For the icing, whisk together the cream cheese, icing sugar and Dulche de Leche. Spoon on top of the cupcakes and sprinkle with the chocolate and pecans. Best eaten the day they are made.

Preparation time: 10 min
Cooking time: 20 min
Serves 16

125g softened butter or margarine
125g soft brown sugar
2 eggs, beaten
150g self-raising flour, sifted
2 over-ripe bananas, mashed
50g pecans, chopped

For the caramel topping:
225g cream cheese
4 tbsp icing sugar, sifted
2–3 tbsp Dulce de Leche
Grated chocolate and chopped
* pecans, to decorate*

Chocolate and sour cherry cupcakes

Preparation time: 20 min
Cooking time: 15 min
Serves 20

150g unsalted butter, softened
150g caster sugar
2 medium eggs, beaten
100g self-raising flour, sifted
50g cocoa powder, sifted
100g dried sour cherries
3 tbsp soured cream

For the cherry icing:
75g butter, softened
175g icing sugar
2–3 tbsp cherry conserve

1. Line 2 x 12-hole cupcake trays with 20 paper cases. Preheat the oven to 350°F (180°C).

2. Whisk the butter and sugar in a bowl until pale and creamy. Whisk in the eggs a little at a time, adding a little flour to prevent the mixture from curdling.

3. Fold in the flour, cocoa powder, cherries and soured cream.

4. Divide between the paper cases and level the tops. Bake for 15 minutes until golden and just firm. Cool for 5 minutes, then transfer to a wire rack to cool completely.

5. Place the butter in a bowl and gradually whisk in the icing sugar. Stir in the cherry conserve to taste, adding a little more icing sugar if necessary. Pipe or spoon on top of the cakes. Best eaten the day they are made.

Coffee and walnut cupcakes

1. Line 2 x 12-hole cupcake trays with 20 paper cases. Preheat the oven to 350°F (180°C). Mix the coffee with 100ml of boiling water and allow to cool.

2. Place the butter, sugar, flour, eggs and 2 tbsp of the coffee in a bowl and whisk with a wooden spoon or electric whisk until pale and creamy. Stir in the chopped walnuts.

3. Divide between the paper cases and level the tops. Bake for 15 minutes until golden and just firm. Cool for 5 minutes, then transfer to a wire rack to cool completely.

4. Whisk together the mascarpone with the icing sugar and remaining coffee, to taste, then pipe or spoon onto the top of the cakes. Top with a walnut half. Best eaten as soon as iced.

Preparation time: 15 min
Cooking time: 15 min
Serves 20

150g unsalted butter, softened
150g light muscovado sugar
150g self-raising flour
2 medium eggs
2 tsp instant coffee powder
50g chopped walnuts

Coffee Icing:
350g mascarpone cheese
4 tbsp icing sugar
20 walnut halves

Cranberry muffins

1. Preheat the oven to 350°F (180°C). Grease a 12-hole muffin tray.

2. Whisk the butter and sugar in a mixing bowl until soft and light. Gradually whisk in the egg until smooth.

3. Sift in the flour, salt, baking powder and bicarbonate of soda and stir into the egg mixture with the yoghurt until just combined. Gently stir in the cranberries.

4. Spoon into the tray and bake for 20–25 minutes until golden and risen. Cool in the tray for a few minutes, then place on a wire rack to cool completely.

5. To decorate: sift the icing sugar into a bowl and stir in the cranberry juice to form a smooth thick icing. Spoon over the muffins and leave to set. Best eaten the day they are made.

Preparation time: 20 min
Cooking time: 25 min
Serves 12

150g butter
150g caster sugar
1 egg
250g plain flour
1 pinch salt
2½ tsp baking powder
½ tsp bicarbonate of soda
300ml plain yoghurt
200g fresh cranberries

To decorate:
200g icing sugar
3–4 tbsp cranberry juice

Pear and anise muffins

1. Preheat the oven to 375°F (190°C). Place 24 paper cases in 2 x 12-hole mini muffin trays.

2. Drain the pears (reserving the juice) and chop into small pieces. Carefully mix the flour with the rolled oats, chopped pears, almonds, lemon zest, ground anise, baking powder and bicarbonate of soda.

3. Lightly whisk the egg in a bowl. Add the sugar, oil, soured cream and 80ml of the pear juice and mix well. Add the dry ingredients to the egg mixture and mix just long enough to moisten the dry ingredients.

4. Spoon into the paper cases and bake for about 15 minutes until springy to the touch. Cool in the trays for 5 minutes, then place on a wire rack to cool completely.

5. To decorate: whisk the cream until thick. Mix with the cream cheese, icing sugar, 2 tbsp pear juice and the lemon zest. Spread roughly on the muffins. Decorate with the star anise and almonds.

Preparation time: 20 min
Cooking time: 15 min
Serves 24 mini muffins

1 can pears (180g drained weight)
100g plain flour
100g rolled oats
50g finely chopped almonds
2 tsp grated lemon zest
1 tsp ground anise
1½ tsp baking powder
½ tsp bicarbonate of soda
1 egg
80g caster sugar
60ml sunflower oil
150ml soured cream

To decorate:
75ml double cream
100g cream cheese
50g icing sugar
2 tsp grated lemon zest
24 whole star anise
whole blanched almonds

Halloween muffins

Preparation time: 20 min
Cooking time: 25 min
Serves 12

250g plain flour
½ tsp bicarbonate of soda
60g chocolate chips
140g caster sugar
1 egg
80ml sunflower oil
250ml buttermilk

For the white icing:
200g icing sugar
1–2 tbsp hot water

For the chocolate icing:
50g icing sugar
2 tbsp cocoa powder
3–4 tbsp warm water

1. Preheat the oven to 350°F (180°C). Grease a 12-hole muffin tray.

2. Mix the dry ingredients together in a bowl. Whisk together the egg, oil and buttermilk in a mixing bowl. Quickly stir in the dry ingredients until just combined. The mixture should be lumpy.

3. Spoon into the trays and bake for 20–25 minutes until risen and golden. Cool in the trays for 5 minutes then place on a wire rack to cool completely.

4. For the white icing, sift the icing sugar into a bowl and stir in enough hot water to make smooth, thick icing. Spread over the muffins.

5. For the chocolate icing, sift the icing sugar and cocoa powder into a bowl. Stir in the water to form smooth, thick icing.

6. Spoon this icing into a piping bag fitted with a fine nozzle. Carefully pipe 4–5 concentric circles onto each muffin. Run a cocktail stick from the centre to the edge of the cake, through each circle of icing, to create a cobweb effect. Alternatively, pipe lines over the circles. Leave to set. Best eaten the day they are made.

Orange and chocolate chip muffins

1. Preheat the oven to 350°F (180°C). Place paper cases in a 12-hole muffin tray.

2. Sift the flour, baking powder and bicarbonate of soda into a bowl. Add the candied orange peel, sugar and half the chocolate chips.

3. Pour the oil into a jug. Add the orange juice, buttermilk and eggs and whisk together with a fork.

4. Pour the wet ingredients into the dry ingradients then gently stir together until just combined.

5. Spoon into the paper cases. Sprinkle over the rest of the chocolate chips and top each muffin with an orange quarter slice.

6. Bake for about 25 minutes until the muffins are risen and firm. Place on a wire rack to cool completely. Best eaten the day they are made.

Preparation time: 15 min
Cooking time: 25 min
Serves 12

300g plain flour
2½ tbsp baking powder
½ tbsp bicarbonate of soda
75g candied orange peel, chopped
100g caster sugar
70g chocolate chips, 60% cocoa
  solids
100ml vegetable oil
100ml orange juice
200ml buttermilk
2 eggs
3 orange slices, quartered

Almond muffins

1. Preheat the oven to 350°F (180°C). Grease a 12-hole muffin tray.

2. Mix together the flour, ground almonds, baking powder and bicarbonate of soda in a bowl.

3. Whisk the eggs lightly in a mixing bowl. Stir in the sugar, oil and soured cream and mix well. Stir in the dry ingredients until just combined.

4. Spoon the mixture into the tins and place 3 flaked almonds on top of each muffin.

5. Bake for about 25 minutes or until golden and risen. Cool the muffins in the tray for 5 minutes, then turn out and place on a wire rack to cool completely. Sift over a little icing sugar just before serving. Serve warm or cold.

Preparation time: 10 min
Cooking time: 25 min
Serves 12

250g plain flour
50g ground almonds
2 tsp baking powder
½ tsp bicarbonate of soda
2 eggs
110g sugar
80ml vegetable oil
250ml soured cream
about 36 flaked almonds
icing sugar, to dust

Muffins with strawberry cream

1. Preheat the oven to 350°F (180°C). Place paper cases in a 12-hole muffin tray.

2. Mix the flour, almonds, baking powder and bicarbonate of soda in a bowl.

3. Whisk the eggs in a separate bowl and stir in the sugar, vanilla extract, oil and soured cream. Add the flour mix to the egg mixture and whisk quickly until all the ingredients are moist.

4. Spoon the mixture into the paper cases. Bake for 20–25 minutes until they turn golden brown. Test using a cocktail stick – if it comes out clean, the muffins are done. Place on a wire rack to cool completely.

5. To decorate: slice 8 strawberries and purée the rest with a hand-held mixer. Pass the purée through a sieve and stir in the icing sugar.

6. Whisk the cream until stiff and fold into the strawberry purée. Pour the strawberry cream into a piping bag with a star-shaped nozzle and top each muffin with the cream.

7. Decorate with strawberry slices and serve at once.

Preparation time: 15 min
Cooking time: 25 min
Serves 12

250g plain flour
50g ground almonds
2 tsp baking powder
½ tsp bicarbonate of soda
3 eggs
100g caster sugar
½ tsp vanilla extract
80ml vegetable oil
250ml soured cream

To decorate:
150g strawberries
1 tbsp icing sugar
150ml double cream

Chocolate marshmallow muffins

1. Preheat the oven to 350°F (180°C). Grease a 12-hole muffin tray.

2. Whisk the egg in a bowl. Cut off the waffle base from each marshmallow and reserve to decorate. Beat the marshmallows with a fork.

3. Add half the marshmallow to the egg. Whisk in the sugar, vanilla, oil and buttermilk. Mix the flour with the baking powder and bicarbonate of soda. Add the flour to the egg mixture and whisk quickly, until the dry ingredients are moist. Spoon the mixture into the tins.

4. Bake for 20–25 minutes. Test with a cocktail stick: if it comes out clean, the muffins are done. Cool in the tin for 5 minutes, then turn out carefully and place on a wire rack to cool completely.

5. To decorate: whisk the mascarpone with the icing sugar. Mix in the remaining marshmallow.

6. Cut the muffins in half horizontally. Spread a little of the marshmallow cream on each muffin base and top with the other half. Spread the rest of the marshmallow cream over the muffins and decorate with the waffle marshmallow bases. Best eaten the day they are made.

Preparation time: 20 min
Cooking time: 25 min
Serves 12

1 egg
12 small chocolate covered
marshmallows, on a waffle base
45g light brown sugar
2 tsp vanilla extract
80ml vegetable oil
250ml buttermilk
250g plain flour
2 ½ tsp baking powder
½ tsp bicarbonate of soda

To decorate:
100g mascarpone, or full-fat cream cheese
2 tbsp icing sugar

Orange marmalade buns with chocolate sauce

1. Preheat the oven to 375°F (190°C). Grease a 12-hole muffin tray.

2. Sift the flour and salt into a bowl and rub in the butter with your fingers until the mixture resembles fine breadcrumbs.

3. Stir in the sugar, followed by the egg and mix well. Add enough milk to give the mixture a soft dropping consistency.

4. Spoon the mixture into the tray and bake for 15–20 minutes until golden and firm. Leave in the trays for 3 minutes, then place on a wire rack to cool completely.

5. For the filling: break up the jelly and put into a bowl with the marmalade and boiling water until the jelly has dissolved. Stir and pour into a large dish or tin to form a 1cm layer of jelly. Leave to cool, then chill until set.

6. When the jelly has set, cut small rounds from it, the same diameter as the cakes. Split the cakes in half through the centre using a sharp knife. Place a jelly disc on top of each flat half and top with the other cake half.

7. Melt the chocolate in a bowl over a pan of simmering (not boiling) water. Spoon over the cakes just before serving.

Preparation time: 20 min
plus chilling
Cooking time: 20 min
Serves 12

225g self-raising flour
pinch salt
110g butter
110g sugar
1 egg, whisked
milk, to mix

For the filling:
135g packet orange jelly
1 tbsp orange marmalade
125ml boiling water

To decorate:
175g dark chocolate

Apple and cinnamon muffins

Preparation time: 20 min
Cooking time: 40 min
Serves 8

125g butter
125g castor sugar
2 large eggs
125g plain flour
1 tsp baking powder
½ tsp bicarbonate of soda
1 tsp ground cinnamon
100ml apple sauce

For the icing
200g icing sugar
5 tbsp milk

To decorate:
1 tsp vanilla extract
1 tsp ground cinnamon
1 apple, quartered, cored
  and chopped

1. Preheat the oven to 350°F (180°C). Grease 8 large muffin tins.

2. Whisk the butter and sugar in a mixing bowl until light and fluffy. Add the eggs, one at a time, beating thoroughly after each addition. Fold in the flour, baking powder, bicarbonate of soda, cinnamon and apple sauce and stir until just combined.

3. Spoon into the tins and bake for 25 minutes until risen and golden.

4. For the icing: sift the icing sugar into a bowl and stir in the milk and vanilla until smooth. If the icing is too stiff, add more milk.

5. Spoon the icing on top of the muffins, allowing it to run down the sides. Sprinkle over the cinnamon and top with apple pieces. Best eaten the day they are made.

Pineapple and coconut muffins

1. Preheat the oven to 350°F (180°C). Grease a 12-hole muffin tray.

2. Sift the flour, baking powder and bicarbonate of soda into a mixing bowl. Stir in the coconut.

3. Lightly whisk together the egg, both sugars, oil, yoghurt and rum. Gently stir into the flour mixture with the pineapple and stir until just combined.

4. Spoon into the tray and bake for 25 minutes until golden and risen. Cool in the tray for 5 minutes, then place on a wire rack to cool completely. Best eaten the day they are made.

Preparation time: 10 min
Cooking time: 25 min
Serves 12

200g plain flour
2 tsp baking powder
½ tsp bicarbonate of soda
50g desiccated coconut
1 egg
50g light brown sugar
100g caster sugar
100ml sunflower oil
250ml plain yoghurt
1–2 tbsp rum
200g crushed pineapple

Strawberry cupcake

1. For the strawberry mousse: put the strawberries in a pan with 100ml water and the sugar. Bring to a boil and simmer for about 3 minutes until the strawberries are soft. Remove from the heat and mash until pulpy. Stir the marshmallows into the hot pulp until they dissolve. Leave to cool.

2. Whisk the cream until it holds its shape, but is not stiff. Fold the cream into the cooled strawberry mixture, then spoon into a bowl and chill for about 2 hours until set.

3. Preheat the oven to 350°F (180°C). Grease a 10-hole muffin tray.

4. Whisk the eggs and sugar until light, then whisk in the cream and vanilla.

5. Sift over the flour and baking powder and fold in lightly, followed by the butter.

6. Fill the tray three-quarters full with the mixture. Bake for 12–15 minutes until golden. Test by lightly pressing the top of the cakes with your fingers – the cakes should spring back. Remove from the oven and leave to cool in the tray for 5 minutes. Turn out onto a wire rack to cool completely.

7. Split each cold cupcake into 3, using a sharp knife. Place a spoonful of the strawberry mousse on one layer and spread fairly thickly over the cake. Top with a layer of cupcake. Spread with another spoonful of mousse and top with the third layer of cake. Chill until ready to serve.

8. To decorate: sift a little icing sugar over the top layer just before serving and top with sliced strawberries.

Preparation time: 20 min
  plus 2 h chilling
Cooking time: 15 min
Serves 10

For the mousse:
250g sliced strawberries
2 tbsp sugar
140g mini marshmallows
200ml double cream

For the cupcakes:
2 eggs
110g caster sugar
50ml double cream
1 tsp vanilla extract
110g self-raising flour
½ tsp baking powder
50g butter, melted

For the decoration:
icing sugar
sliced strawberries

Chocolate hazelnut cupcake

1. Preheat the oven to 400°F (200°C). Place paper cases in a 12-hole muffin tray.

2. Put the hazelnuts in a mixing bowl and sift in the icing sugar and flour. Stir in the egg whites and grated chocolate.

3. Spoon into the paper cases and bake for 15–20 minutes until golden. Leave in the tins for 5 minutes, then place on a wire rack to cool completely.

4. Reduce the oven temperature to 350°F (180°C).

5. For the chocolate meringue: line a large baking tray with non-stick paper. Whisk the egg whites and cream of tartar in a bowl until soft peaks form, then gradually whisk in the sugar, 1 tablespoon at a time, until stiff and glossy. Sift in the cocoa powder and gently fold into the egg whites.

6. Spoon rounds of the meringue (the same size as the cakes) onto the baking tray. Put them into the oven, then immediately turn the heat down to its lowest setting. Bake for about 45 minutes–1 hour until crisp on the outside. Place on a wire rack to cool.

7. For the topping: beat the butter and cocoa powder until combined. Gradually sift in the icing sugar and whisk well until smooth.

8. Spread a little of the topping on each cake and top with a disc of meringue.

Preparation time: 25 min
Cooking time: 1 h 10 min
Serves 12

175g ground hazelnuts
175g icing sugar
75g plain flour
5 egg whites
50g grated plain chocolate, 70%
  cocoa solids

For the chocolate meringue:
3 egg whites
$1/_8$ tsp cream of tartar
125g caster sugar
1 tbsp cocoa powder

For the chocolate topping:
110g butter
2 tbsp cocoa powder, sifted
150g icing sugar

Tiramisu cupcake

Preparation time: 15 min
Cooking time: 20 min
Serves 12

110g butter, softened
110g light brown sugar
110g self-raising flour
1 tbsp cocoa powder
1 tbsp espresso coffee powder
2 large eggs
1–2 tbsp milk

For the topping:
300ml double cream
2 tbsp icing sugar, sifted
4 tbsp cocoa powder

1. Preheat the oven to 350°F (180°C). Place paper cases in a 12-hole muffin tray.

2. Mix all the cake ingredients in a mixing bowl until smooth and creamy. Add more milk if the mixture is too stiff.

3. Spoon into the paper cases and bake for 18–20 minutes until springy to the touch. Cool for 5 minutes in the tray, then place on a wire rack to cool completely.

4. For the topping: whisk the cream and icing sugar until thick. Spoon into a piping bag and pipe on top of the cakes. Sift cocoa powder over the top just before serving.

Toffee cupcake

1. Preheat the oven to 400°F (200°C). Place paper cases in a 12-hole muffin tray.

2. Sift the flour, sugar, baking powder and salt into a mixing bowl. Whisk together the egg, milk, oil and vanilla. Stir into the dry ingredients until combined.

3. Spoon into the paper cases and bake for about 20 minutes until golden and risen. Cool in the tin for 5 minutes, then place on a wire rack to cool completely.

4. For the toffee cream: heat the sugar, water, and salt in a pan over medium heat, stirring once, until the sugar is dissolved. Continue cooking, but do not stir, until the sugar turns golden amber. Remove from the heat.

5. Slowly pour the cream into the pan – it will spatter. Heat gently, stirring until combined. Pour the toffee cream into a mixing bowl and leave to cool. Chill for about 40 minutes until cold, stirring occasionally.

6. For the caramel sauce: put the sugar in a heavy-based frying pan and stir in the water. Heat gently, tilting the pan, (do not stir or the sugar will crystallise) until the sugar has dissolved. Increase the heat and bubble for 4–5 minutes until golden brown. Remove from the heat, and carefully stir in the cream and butter. Pour into a jug or bowl and leave to cool.

7. Whisk the toffee cream until soft peaks form. Spoon into a piping bag and pipe on top of the cold buns. Drizzle with the caramel sauce and top with a sultana.

Preparation time: 25 min
plus 40 min chilling
Cooking time: 30 min
Serves 12

225g plain flour
110g castor sugar
2 tsp baking powder
pinch salt
1 egg, whisked
150ml milk
50ml sunflower oil
1 tsp vanilla extract

For the toffee cream:
110g sugar
2 tbsp water
pinch salt
400ml double cream

For the caramel sauce:
250g caster sugar
4 tbsp water
150ml double cream
50g butter

To decorate:
12 sultanas

Mixed berry cupcake

1. Preheat the oven to 375°F (190°C). Grease a 12-hole fluted bun tin with butter or use a silicone mould.

2. Mix the melted butter with the rosewater. Place the ground almonds in a mixing bowl and sift in the icing sugar and flour.

3. Whisk the egg whites lightly to combine and stir into the dry ingredients. Add the melted butter mixture and mix gently until combined.

4. Pour into the tin and bake for about 15 minutes (depending on the size of the tin or mould) until springy to the touch. Cool in the tin for a few minutes then place on a wire rack to cool completely.

5. For the mixed berry sauce: heat the sugar and water in a pan over a low heat until the sugar has dissolved. Add the mixed berries, bring to the boil and simmer for 5 minutes until the berries are still whole and the sauce has thickened. Stir in the rosewater.

6. Pour a little of the sauce over and around each cake, so that the cakes are soaked in the sauce.

7. Whisk the cream until thick and spoon or pipe a swirl on top of each cake. Top with a little more sauce and berries.

Preparation time: 15 min
Cooking time: 15 min
Serves 12

175g butter, melted
1 tsp rosewater
125g ground almonds
225g icing sugar
9 tbsp plain flour
6 egg whites

For the sauce:
200g caster sugar
200ml water
400g fresh or frozen mixed
    summer berries
1 tsp rosewater

To decorate:
300ml double cream

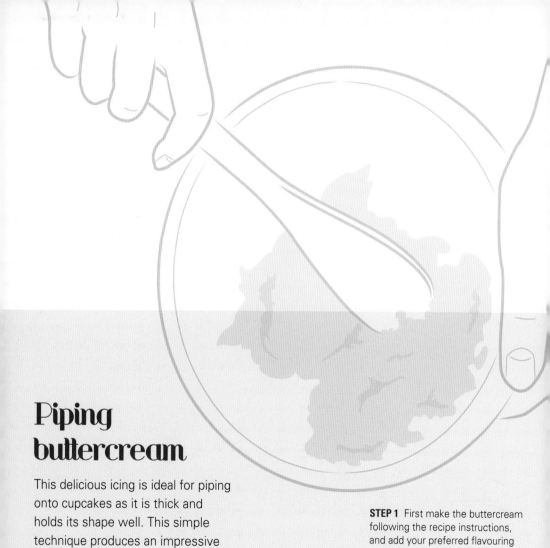

Piping buttercream

This delicious icing is ideal for piping onto cupcakes as it is thick and holds its shape well. This simple technique produces an impressive and indulgent result.

STEP 1 First make the buttercream following the recipe instructions, and add your preferred flavouring or colouring.

STEP 2 Either prepare your icing bag or cut the corner off a plastic bag to create a hole the right size for piping.

STEP 3 With the nozzle in place (if you are using a piping bag), spoon in the icing until the bag is about half full.

STEP 4 Twist the open end of the bag to create a firm bag of icing. Hold the top with one hand and the lower end with the other.

STEP 5 Starting from the outside edge of the cakes, squeeze the bag gently and steadily and swirl the icing around the top of the cakes.

Mini flower cupcakes with white chocolate icing

1. Preheat the oven to 350°F (180°C). Place paper cases in 2 x 12 mini cupcake trays.

2. Whisk the butter and sugar until light and creamy. Gradually whisk in the eggs until well blended. Sift in the flour and fold in gently with the vanilla, until just combined.

3. Spoon into the paper cases and bake for 10–15 minutes until golden and springy to the touch. Place on a wire rack to cool completely.

4. For the white chocolate icing: melt the chocolate in a heatproof bowl over a pan of simmering (not boiling) water, stirring once. Leave to cool.

5. Whisk the butter and icing sugar in a bowl until creamy. Whisk in the melted chocolate until smooth.

6. Spread over the cakes and leave to set. Sift over a little icing sugar and decorate each with a white flower.

Preparation time: 15 min
Cooking time: 15 min
Serves 24 mini cakes

110g butter
110g caster sugar
2 eggs, whisked
110g self-raising flour
1 tsp vanilla extract

For the white chocolate icing:
100g white chocolate
140g unsalted butter
140g icing sugar

To decorate:
icing sugar
24 white flowers

Pistachio and white chocolate cupcakes

1. Preheat the oven to 375°F (190°C). Place paper cases in a 12-hole muffin tray.

2. Mix the ground pistachios, icing sugar and flour in a mixing bowl. Add the egg whites and stir until blended. Stir in the melted butter.

3. Pour into the paper cases and bake for 15–20 minutes until golden and springy to the touch. Sprinkle the sugar over the top of the warm cakes. Cool in the tray for 5 minutes then place on a wire rack to cool completely.

4. To decorate: scatter the sugar and pistachios over the top of the cakes and drizzle with white chocolate.

Preparation time: 15 min
Cooking time: 20 min
Serves 12

110g ground pistachios
225g icing sugar
75g plain flour
6 egg whites, lightly whisked
175g butter
4 tbsp sugar

To decorate:
6 tbsp sugar
100g chopped pistachios
75g white chocolate, melted

Rhubarb muffins

1. Preheat the oven to 400°F (200°C). Place paper cases in a 12-hole muffin tray.

2. Mix the rhubarb with the sugar. Bake the rhubarb for about 10 minutes until just tender. Drain well and set aside to cool.

3. Mix the flour with the baking powder and cinnamon in a mixing bowl.

4. Whisk the eggs with the milk and melted butter. Mix with the dry ingredients with the rhubarb until just combined. The mixture will be lumpy.

5. Spoon into the paper cases and sprinkle the tops with demerara sugar. Bake for 25–30 minutes until risen and golden. Place on a wire rack to cool completely.

Preparation time: 15 min
Cooking time: 40 min
Serves 12

*1–2 small sticks of rhubarb
  (about 300g)*
3 tbsp sugar
300g plain flour
1 tsp baking powder
100g caster sugar
1 tsp ground cinnamon
2 eggs, whisked
200ml milk
100g butter, melted
2–3 tbsp demerara sugar

Cupcakes with marzipan roses

Preparation time: 25 min
Cooking time: 20 min
Serves 12

225g plain flour
90g caster sugar
2 tsp baking powder
1 pinch salt
1 egg, whisked
150ml milk
50ml sunflower oil
1 tsp almond extract

For the topping:
icing sugar
225g lilac sugar paste
225g white sugar paste

For the royal icing:
1 egg white
250g icing sugar

To decorate:
6 lilac marzipan roses
6 white marzipan roses

1. Preheat the oven to 400°F (200°C). Place paper cases in a 12-hole muffin tray.

2. Sift the flour, sugar, baking powder and salt into a mixing bowl.

3. Whisk together the egg, milk, oil and almond extract. Stir into the dry ingredients until combined.

4. Spoon into the paper cases and bake for about 20 minutes until golden and risen. Cool in the tray for 5 minutes, then place on a wire rack to cool completely.

5. For the topping: dust a surface with icing sugar and roll out the lilac sugar paste thinly. Cut into 6 rounds the same diameter as the cakes. Repeat with the white sugar paste.

6. Brush 1 side of the sugar paste rounds with a little water and place on top of the cakes, pressing and smoothing to remove any air bubbles.

7. For the icing: place the egg white in a bowl. Sift in the icing sugar, then stir to make a thick, smooth icing. The icing should stand in firm peaks. Spoon into a piping bag and pipe lines and dots on the sugar paste, as in the photo.

8. Place a marzipan rose on top of each cake before the icing sets.

Pistachio and almond cupcakes

1. Preheat the oven to 325°F (160°C). Place paper cases in a 12-hole muffin tray.

2. Mix together the pistachios, sugar, butter, eggs, flour and milk in a mixing bowl until smooth.

3. Spoon into the paper cases and bake for 20–25 minutes until golden and springy to the touch. Place on a wire rack to cool completely.

4. For the icing: mix just enough water into the icing sugar to get a very thick icing. Stir in the vanilla.

5. Spread the icing on the cakes and sprinkle with the ground pistachios.

6. Line a tray with non-stick baking paper. Melt the chocolate in a heatproof bowl over a pan of simmering (not boiling) water. Spoon 12 'horseshoe' shapes onto the paper and leave to set. Place the chocolate shapes on top of the cupcakes.

Preparation time: 20 min
Cooking time: 25 min
Serves 12

85g finely chopped pistachios
150g caster sugar
150g butter
2 eggs
150g self-raising flour
5 tbsp milk

For the icing:
250g icing sugar, sifted
2–3 tbsp water
few drops vanilla extract

To decorate:
120g ground pistachios
110g finely chopped chocolate

Confetti cupcakes with mandarin orange segments

1. Preheat the oven to 350°F (180°C). Place paper cases in a 12-hole cupcake tray.

2. Whisk the butter and sugar until light and fluffy. Gradually whisk in the eggs until blended. Sift in the flour and beat well. Stir in the orange flowerwater and cream.

3. Spoon into the paper cases and bake for 20–25 minutes until golden and risen. Cool in the tray for 5 minutes, then place on a wire rack to cool completely.

4. For the decoration: whisk the cream until thick. Stir in the icing sugar. Split the vanilla pod and scrape out the seeds into the cream. Stir well.

5. Spoon the cream into a piping bag and pipe on top of the cakes. Decorate with candied orange peel and place a mandarin orange segment on each cake.

Preparation time: 20 min
Cooking time: 25 min
Serves 12

225g butter
225g caster sugar
4 eggs, whisked
225g self-raising flour
1 tsp orange flowerwater
1 tbsp double cream

For the decoration:
300ml double cream
1–2 tbsp icing sugar
1 vanilla pod
75g candied orange peel, chopped
12 mandarin orange segments

Vanilla coffee cupcakes

1. Preheat the oven to 350°F (180°C). Place paper cases in a 12-hole cupcake tray.

2. Whisk the sugar and butter in a mixing bowl until creamy. Gradually beat in the eggs and cream.

3. Sift in the instant coffee, flour and baking powder and stir into the mixture with the ground almonds and salt until just combined.

4. Spoon into the paper cases and bake for 25 minutes until risen and springy to the touch.

5. For the coffee syrup: split the vanilla pod lengthways and scrape out the paste. Put into a pan with the espresso, vanilla pod and sugar and heat slowly. Bring to a boil and simmer for 5 minutes. Set aside to cool. Remove the vanilla pod. Drizzle the warm cakes with the syrup and leave to cool.

6. To decorate: whisk the cream with the icing sugar and vanilla until stiff and spoon into a piping bag. Pipe swirls on top of the cakes and place a raspberry on each cake.

Preparation time: 20 min
Cooking time: 25 min
Serves 12

150g caster sugar
150g butter
3 eggs
100ml double cream
1 ½ tbsp instant coffee powder
150g plain flour
1 tsp baking powder
50g ground almonds
pinch salt

For the coffee syrup:
1 vanilla pod
100ml freshly made espresso coffee
70g sugar

To decorate:
200ml double cream
1 tbsp icing sugar
½ tsp vanilla extract
12 raspberries

Rose and lychee cupcakes

Preparation time: 20 min
Cooking time: 25 min
Serves 12

180ml puréed lychees, skinned and pitted
60ml milk
½ tsp vanilla extract
110g butter
200g caster sugar
1 egg
2 egg whites
200g plain flour
1 tsp baking powder
¼ tsp salt

For the buttercream:
140g unsalted butter
110g icing sugar, sifted
2 tsp milk
½ tsp rose water
2–3 drops pink colouring

For the decoration:
rose petals

1. Preheat the oven to 350°F (180°C) gas 4. Place 12 cupcake cases in a cupcake tray.

2. Mix the puréed lychees with the milk and vanilla extract.

3. Mix the butter and sugar until soft and light. Add the egg and egg whites and mix until blended. Sift in the flour, baking powder and salt and stir until combined. Add the lychee and milk mixture and mix until just combined.

4. Spoon the mixture into the paper cases and bake for 20–25 minutes until the tops are lightly golden and spring back to the touch. Leave to cool in the tray for 10 minutes, then place on a wire rack to cool completely.

5. For the buttercream: whisk the butter until very soft and creamy. Gradually whisk in the icing sugar and milk, followed by the rose water and colouring and whisk until smooth.

6. Pipe or spoon the frosting onto the cupcakes and top each with a rose petal.

Gingerbread muffin

1. Preheat the oven to 350°F (180°C). Place paper cases in a 12-hole muffin tray.

2. Sift the flour, sugar, baking powder and spices into a mixing bowl.

3. Whisk together the eggs, honey and butter until smooth. Stir into the dry ingredients.

4. Add enough water to give a soft droppping consistency and stir well until combined.

5. Spoon into the paper cases and bake for 20–25 minutes until golden and a skewer inserted into the centre comes out clean. Leave in the tray for 5 minutes, then place on a wire rack to cool completely.

6. Sift a little icing sugar over each muffin, then sift over a little ground ginger.

Preparation time: 10 min
Cooking time: 25 min
Serves 12

250g plain flour
225g light brown sugar
2 tsp baking powder
2 tsp ground ginger
½ tsp ground cinnamon
½ tsp ground mixed spice
1 pinch ground cloves
2 eggs
100ml clear honey
110g butter, melted
125–175ml hot water

To decorate:
3 tbsp icing sugar
3 tbsp ground ginger

Apple muffins

1. Preheat the oven to 375°F (190°C). Place paper cases in a 12-hole muffin tray.

2. Place the flour, sugar, baking powder and 1 teaspoon cinnamon into a mixing bowl.

3. Add the egg, milk, apples and oil and stir for a few seconds until just combined. Spoon the mixture into the paper cases.

4. Mix together the pecan nuts, brown sugar and the rest of the cinnamon. Sprinkle over each muffin. Bake for 15–20 minutes until well risen and firm. Place on a wire rack to cool.

Preparation time: 10 min
Cooking time: 20 min
Serves 12

225g plain flour
75g caster sugar
2 tsp baking powder
2 tsp ground cinnamon
1 egg
150ml milk
2 apples, peeled, cored and finely chopped
50ml sunflower oil
2 tbsp pecan nuts, finely chopped
50g light brown sugar

Baking cupcakes

The trick for getting the perfect finish for your cupcakes is in how you fill the cases. When it comes to baking, less is definitely more! Too much and you'll be slicing off the tops, too little and you'll be trimming the paper cases.

STEP 1 Fill the muffin tray with paper cases. Using a spatula and a teaspoon, half-fill the cases with cake mixture.

STEP 2 Once all the cases have mixture in them, carefully level off the tops without pressing down too much and expelling all the air.

STEP 3 Bake the cupcakes in the oven according to the recipe instructions, or until the tops spring back when lightly pressed with your fingers.

STEP 4 Leave the cakes in the tray until cool enough to handle, then transfer to a wire rack to cool completely.

STEP 5 When the cakes are completely cold, ice each one in turn, either by spreading or piping the icing on top.

Lemon and poppy seed muffins

1. Preheat the oven to 350°F (180°C). Place paper cases in a 12-hole muffin tray.

2. Mix the flour, sugar, lemon zest and poppy seeds together in a mixing bowl.

3. Whisk the eggs with the yoghurt, then add to the dry ingredients with the melted butter. Mix together until smooth.

4. Spoon into the paper cases and bake for 20–25 minutes until risen and springy to the touch. The cakes will be quite pale on top.

5. Cool in the tray for 5 minutes, then place on a wire rack to cool completely.

6. Sift over a little icing sugar just before serving.

Preparation time: 10 min
Cooking time: 25 min
Serves 12

225g self-raising flour
175g caster sugar
2 lemons, finely grated zest
1 tbsp poppy seeds, toasted
3 eggs
100ml plain yoghurt
175g butter, melted
icing sugar, to dust

Chocolate muffins

1. Preheat the oven to 400°F (200°C). Place paper cases in a 12-hole muffin tray.

2. Sift the flour, baking powder and salt into a mixing bowl. Stir in the sugar.

3. Melt the chocolate and butter in a heatproof bowl over a pan of simmering (not boiling) water. Remove from the heat and stir into the flour mixture.

4. Add the eggs and vanilla to the mixture and stir until only just combined.

5. Spoon into the paper cases and bake for 20–25 minutes until well risen and firm. Cool in the tray for 5 minutes, then place on a wire rack to cool completely.

6. For the icing: sift the icing sugar into a bowl and gradually stir in the lemon juice, water and a few drops of colouring until smooth and very thick.

7. Place a spoonful of icing in the centre of each cake. Place a mini chocolate egg on top of the icing and leave to set.

Preparation time: 10 min
Cooking time: 25 min
Serves 12

110g plain flour
1 tbsp baking powder
pinch salt
175g caster sugar
110g dark chocolate, 60% cocoa solids
225g butter
4 eggs, whisked
1 tsp vanilla extract

For the icing:
175g icing sugar
2 tbsp lemon juice
1 tsp hot water
yellow food colouring

To decorate:
12 mini chocolate eggs

Peanut muffins with crispy topping

1. Preheat the oven to 350°F (180°C). Place paper cases in a 12-hole muffin tray.

2. Sift the flour, sugar, baking powder and salt into a mixing bowl.

3. Whisk the eggs, milk, oil, butter and peanut butter together until combined and stir into the dry ingredients until just mixed. The mixture should be slightly lumpy.

4. Spoon into the paper cases and bake for 20–25 minutes until golden and risen. Cool in the tray for 5 minutes, then place on a wire rack to cool completely.

5. For the peanut buttercream: whisk the peanut butter and butter with an electric whisk until smooth. Add the sugar and whisk until fluffy.

6. For the crispy peanut topping: line a baking sheet with non-stick baking paper. Heat the sugar in a pan until melted and amber coloured. Do not stir. Remove from the heat and add the peanuts, stirring well. Pour onto the baking sheet. Leave to cool and set for a few minutes, then break up into pieces.

7. Spoon the peanut butter cream on top of the muffins. Decorate with the crispy peanut pieces.

Preparation time: 20 min
Cooking time: 25 min
Serves 12

275g plain flour
175g caster sugar
1 tbsp baking powder
1 pinch salt
2 eggs
175ml milk
50ml sunflower oil
50g butter, melted

For the peanut buttercream:
110g smooth peanut butter
150g smooth peanut butter
110g butter
100g icing sugar

For the crispy peanut topping:
200g sugar
175g unsalted peanuts, lightly crushed

Apricot and ginger muffins

Preparation time: 15 min
Cooking time: 30 min
Serves 6

150g plain flour
½ tbsp baking powder
1 egg
50g caster sugar
110ml milk
50g butter, melted
1 tsp vanilla extract
110g chopped fresh apricots

For the topping:
75g butter
2 tbsp golden syrup
120g icing sugar
75g chopped stem ginger

1. Preheat the oven to 400°F (200°C). Grease a 6-hole muffin tray.

2. Sift the flour, baking powder and salt into a mixing bowl.

3. Mix together the egg, sugar, milk, butter and vanilla. Stir into the dry ingredients quickly until only just combined and still slightly lumpy.

4. Gently fold in the apricots.

5. Spoon into the tray almost to the top and bake for 25–30 minutes until risen and golden.

6. For the topping: heat the butter, golden syrup and icing sugar in a small pan over a medium heat for about 5 minutes until smooth. Stir in the ginger.

7. Spoon on top of the partially cooked muffins for the last 5–8 minutes of cooking time.

8. When the muffins are cooked and the topping is crisp, leave in the tins for 5 minutes. Place on a wire rack to cool completely.

Pear muffins with crispy flaked almonds

1. Preheat the oven to 350°F (180°C) and grease an 8-hole muffin tray.

2. Mix the butter and sugar together in a mixing bowl until light, then add the eggs, one at a time, whisking well.

3. Add the flour, baking powder and ground almonds to the cake mixture and fold in until smooth.

4. Spoon the mixture into the tins to cover the base. Stand 4 pear quarters in each tin and carefully spoon the mixture over and around the pears.

5. Bake for 20 minutes, until the pears are soft and the muffins are cooked through. Cool in the tins for 5 minutes, then place on a wire rack to cool completely.

6. For the crispy almond topping: lightly oil a baking tray. Heat the sugar and water in a pan over a medium heat, swirling the pan from time to time until the sugar dissolves.

7. Lower the heat to very low and simmer gently until the liquid forms a pale golden caramel. Tip in the toasted almonds and cook gently for 2–3 minutes until the caramel is a light golden colour, then immediately pour onto the oiled tray and set aside to cool and harden.

8. When the caramel has set, break into pieces and place on the muffins.

Preparation time: 15 min
Cooking time: 20 min
Serves 8

125g butter
125g caster sugar
3 eggs
150g self-raising flour
1 tsp baking powder
25g ground almonds
8 small pears, peeled, cored and
*   quartered*

For the crispy almonds:
200g flaked almonds, lightly toasted
110g caster sugar
2 tbsp water

Macadamia and chocolate muffins

1. Preheat the oven to 350°F (180°C). Place paper cases in a 12-hole muffin tray.

2. Melt the chocolate and butter in a heatproof bowl over a pan of simmering (not boiling) water.

3. Whisk together the sugar, milk, egg and soured cream in a mixing bowl until smooth.

4. Sift in the flour, cornflour, baking powder, cocoa and salt and stir in with the melted chocolate until blended. Spoon into the paper cases and sprinkle the chocolate chips and nuts on top.

5. Bake for 25–30 minutes until risen and firm. Cool in the tray for 10 minutes, then place on a wire rack to cool completely.

Preparation time: 15 min
Cooking time: 30 min
Serves 12

75g plain chocolate
100g butter
100g caster sugar
200ml milk
1 egg
100ml soured cream
200g plain flour
2 tsp cornflour
1 tbsp baking powder
3 tbsp cocoa powder
pinch salt
75g chocolate chips
75g chopped macadamia nuts

Banana and walnut muffin

1. Preheat the oven to 375°F (190°C). Place paper cases in a 12-hole muffin tray.

2. Sift the flour, baking powder, bicarbonate of soda and salt into a mixing bowl, then add the sugar.

3. Whisk together the eggs, vanilla extract, butter and milk until combined.

4. Mash the bananas well and stir into the egg mixture.

5. Make a well in the centre of the dry ingredients and add the egg mixture with the walnuts, stirring roughly with a fork (don't over mix) until it is a lumpy paste.

6. Spoon the mixture into the paper cases and bake for 20–25 minutes until the muffins are golden and risen and springy to the touch. Cool in the tray for 5 minutes then place on a wire rack to cool completely.

7. To decorate: whisk the cream until thick. Spoon into a piping bag and pipe a little cream on top of the muffins. Drizzle with a little honey.

Preparation time: 10 min
Cooking time: 25 min
Serves 12

250g self-raising flour
1 tsp baking powder
½ tsp bicarbonate of soda
pinch salt
110g caster sugar
2 eggs
1 tsp vanilla extract
75g butter, melted
125ml milk
2 large ripe bananas
110g chopped walnuts

To decorate:
200ml double cream
60ml runny honey

Apple muffins with walnut caramel

Preparation time: 15 min
Cooking time: 25 min
Serves 12

250g plain flour
225g caster sugar
1 tbsp baking powder
1 tsp ground cinnamon
110ml sunflower oil
2 eggs
175ml milk
1 apple, peeled and diced

For the caramel topping:
75g butter
2 tbsp sugar
2 tbsp water
3 apples, peeled and thickly sliced
75g walnuts, halved

1. Preheat the oven to 350°F (180°C). Grease a 12-hole muffin tin.

2. Sift the flour, sugar, baking powder and cinnamon into a mixing bowl.

3. Mix together the oil, eggs and milk until combined. Stir into the dry ingredients until only just combined but still lumpy. Gently fold in the apple.

4. Spoon into the tins and bake for 20–25 minutes until golden and risen. Leave in the tins for 2 minutes then place on a wire rack to cool.

5. For the topping: heat the butter, sugar and water in a pan until the sugar has dissolved. Bring to a boil. Add the apple slices and walnuts. Cook for 2–3 minutes, until the apples are soft and coated with syrup.

6. Invert the muffins onto a plate and spoon over the topping. Serve warm.

Pineapple, coconut and carrot muffins

1. Preheat the oven to 350°F (180°C). Line a 12-hole muffin tray with paper muffin cases.

2. Sift together the flour, cinnamon, mixed spice and baking powder. Stir in the sugar, carrots, coconut, raisins, nuts and pineapple.

3. Whisk together the eggs, oil, soured cream and vanilla extract. Pour into the dry ingredients and stir together until just combined.

4. Spoon the mixture into the paper cases and bake for 20 minutes until risen and firm.

5. To decorate: brush the tops of the warm muffins with most of the honey. Sprinkle over the coconut and hazelnuts and return to the oven for 5 minutes, to lightly brown the coconut. Place on a wire rack to cool completely.

6. Dip the tip of the pineapple pieces into the remaining honey and place on top of each muffin.

Preparation time: 25 min
Cooking time: 20 min
Serves 12

225g plain flour
1 tsp ground cinnamon
1 tsp mixed spice
1 tbsp baking powder
225g caster sugar
110g grated carrots
150g dessicated coconut
100g raisins
75g chopped hazelnuts
1 x 200g crushed pineapple, drained
2 eggs
150ml vegetable oil
150ml soured cream
1 tsp vanilla extract

To decorate:
3 tbsp runny honey, warmed
4 tbsp shredded coconut
2 tbsp chopped hazelnuts
24 pieces glacé pineapple

Lemon muffin soaked in syrup

1. Preheat the oven to 400°F (200°C). Grease a 12-hole muffin tray.

2. Sift the flour and baking powder into a mixing bowl and stir in the sugar. Stir in the grated butter to coat in the flour mixture.

3. Whisk together the egg and milk and pour into the dry ingredients. Mix until just combined. The mixture will be lumpy. Gently fold in the blueberries and raspberries.

4. Spoon into the tins. Bake for 20–25 minutes until the muffins are risen and golden. Sprinkle lightly with a little extra sugar while still warm.

5. For the lemon syrup: put all the syrup ingredients in a small pan and bring to a boil. Cover the pan and and boil gently for 5 minutes.

6. Invert the warm muffins onto serving plates and spoon over the hot syrup.

7. Whisk the cream, icing sugar and vanilla until thick and spoon on top of each muffin. Place a strip of pared lemon zest on top of the cream. Serve with a few fresh raspberries.

Preparation time: 20 min
Cooking time: 25 min
Serves 12

250g plain flour
1 tbsp baking powder
110g caster sugar, plus extra
75g chilled butter, grated
1 large egg
175ml milk
150g mixed blueberries and
    raspberries, lightly crushed

For the lemon syrup:
110g sugar
150ml water
50ml lemon juice
1 lemon, finely grated zest

For the decoration:
300ml double cream
1–2 tbsp icing sugar
1 tsp vanilla extract
1 lemon, pared zest
fresh raspberries (optional)

Raspberry muffins

1. Preheat the oven to 350°F (180°C). Grease a 12-hole muffin tray.

2. Mix the butter and sugar in a mixing bowl until pale and fluffy. Mix in the lemon zest, eggs, vanilla and salt.

3. Sift in the flour and baking powder and stir into the creamed mixture alternately with the milk.

4. Gently fold in the raspberries.

5. Spoon the mixture into the paper cases and bake for about 20–30 minutes until golden and risen. Cool in the tray for a few minutes then place on a wire rack to cool completely.

Preparation time: 10 min
Cooking time: 30 min
Serves 12

100g butter
175g caster sugar
1 tbsp grated lemon zest
2 eggs
1 tsp vanilla extract
pinch salt
250g plain flour
2 tsp baking powder
150ml milk
225g fresh raspberries

Chocolate chilli muffins

1. Preheat the oven to 400°F (200°C). Place paper cases in a 12-hole muffin tray.

2. Sift the flour, cocoa, baking powder and chilli powder into a mixing bowl. Stir in the sugar.

3. Whisk together the eggs and oil in a separate bowl until frothy, then slowly whisk in the milk.

4. Stir into the dry ingredients until just blended. The mixture will be slightly lumpy. Gently stir in the chocolate.

5. Spoon into the paper cases and bake for 20 minutes until risen and springy to the touch. Cool in the tins for 5 minutes then place on a wire rack to cool completely.

Preparation time: 10 min
Cooking time: 20 min
Serves 12

200g plain flour
25g cocoa powder
1 tbsp baking powder
½ tsp chilli powder
110g caster sugar
2 eggs
100ml sunflower oil
225ml milk
75g finely chopped chilli-flavoured chocolate

Apple and berry muffins with crumble topping

1. Preheat the oven to 350°F (180°C). Place paper cases in a 12-hole muffin tray.

2. Mix the flour, baking powder, bicarbonate of soda, cinnamon, apples and blueberries in a mixing bowl.

3. Whisk together the egg, sugar, oil, vanilla and buttermilk and mix well.

4. Stir into the dry ingredients and mix until just combined.

5. For the streusel topping: mix all the topping ingredients with your hands to form a crumble.

6. Spoon the mixture into the paper cases and sprinkle the crumble on top.

7. Bake for 25–30 minutes until golden. Cool in the tray for 5 minutes, then place on a wire rack to cool completely.

8. Sift over a little icing sugar just before serving.

Preparation time: 10 min
Cooking time: 30 min
Serves 12

250g plain flour
2 ½ tsp baking powder
½ tsp bicarbonate of soda
2 tsp ground cinnamon
200g grated apples, mixed with
   1 tbsp lemon juice mixed
100g blueberries
1 egg
140g caster sugar
80ml vegetable oil
250ml buttermilk

For the streusel topping:
50g flour
30g ground almonds
75g sugar
1 tsp ground cinnamon
90g butter
icing sugar, for dusting

Chocolate whisky cakes with blackberry compote

Preparation time: 20 min
Cooking time: 30 min
Serves 10

110g butter
75g caster sugar
2 tbsp light brown sugar
2 eggs
175g plain flour
1 tsp baking powder
120ml whisky
75g chocolate chips

For the blackberry compote:
50ml blackberry liqueur
50g sugar
250g blackberries

To decorate:
icing sugar

1. Preheat the oven to 375°F (190°C). Grease a 10-hole muffin tray.

2. Whisk the butter until light, then mix in the caster sugar and light brown sugar until fluffy.

3. Whisk in the eggs until combined. Sift in the flour and baking powder and fold into the mixture, followed by the whisky and chocolate chips.

4. Spoon into the tray and bake for 25 minutes until golden and risen. Leave in the tray for 5 minutes then place on a wire rack to cool completely.

5. For the blackberry compote: heat the sugar and liqueur in a pan until the sugar has dissolved and simmer for 2 minutes.

6. Add the blackberries and simmer for a further 2–3 minutes, until the blackberries are tender, but still whole and the mixture has just thickened.

7. Place the cakes on serving plates. Spoon a little blackberry compote alongside each cake. Sift a little icing sugar over the cakes.

Banana cupcakes with Dulce de Leche topping

1. Preheat the oven to 400°F (200°C). Place paper cases in a 12-hole cupcake tray.

2. Mash the bananas. Whisk the eggs with the vanilla, butter and sugar in a mixing bowl until light and fluffy. Mix in the banana.

3. Sift in the flour and baking powder and lightly mix, until just combined.

4. Spoon into the paper cases and bake for about 25 minutes until golden and risen. Cool in the tin for 5 minutes, then place on a wire rack to cool completely.

5. Spoon a little Dulce de Leche in the centre of each cake and place a chocolate heart on top.

Preparation time: 15 min
Cooking time: 25 min
Serves 12

2 ripe bananas
3 eggs
1 tsp vanilla extract
150g butter
150g caster sugar
150g plain flour
1 tsp baking powder

To decorate:
6 tbsp Dulce de Leche
12 chocolate hearts

Curry muffins with mango chutney

1. Preheat the oven to 400°F (200°C). Place paper cases in an 8-hole muffin tray.

2. Mix the flour, sugar, baking powder, bicarbonate of soda, salt and curry powder in a mixing bowl. Stir in the raisins, mango and coconut.

3. Whisk together the egg, buttermilk and melted butter in a separate bowl. Quickly stir into the dry ingredients until just combined. The mixture will be lumpy.

4. Spoon the mixture into the paper cases and bake for 15–20 minutes until risen and lightly browned. Serve warm with mango chutney.

Preparation time: 10 min
Cooking time: 20 min
Serves 8

75g plain flour
50g caster sugar
1 tsp baking powder
¼ tsp bicarbonate of soda
pinch salt
1 tsp curry powder
50g raisins
50g dried mango, thinly sliced
40g desiccated coconut
1 egg
110ml buttermilk
2 tbsp butter, melted

To serve:
mango chutney

Pumpkin and bacon muffins

1. Preheat the oven to 350°F (180°C). Grease a 12-hole muffin tin.

2. Mix the flour, baking powder, curry powder and Parmesan in a mixing bowl. Stir in the bacon and pumpkin.

3. Whisk the eggs with the oil and soured cream. Stir the egg mixture into the dry ingredients until just combined. Spoon into the tray and bake for about 30 minutes until golden brown.

4. Serve warm garnished with fried pumpkin slices and fried bacon.

Preparation time: 10 min
Cooking time: 30 min
Serves 12

250g plain flour
2 tsp baking powder
½ tsp curry powder
100g grated Parmesan
100g cooked bacon, diced
250g diced pumpkin flesh
2 eggs
70ml olive oil
200ml soured cream

To serve:
cooked bacon
fried pumpkin strips

Mozzarella and tomato muffin

Preparation time: 15 min
Cooking time: 20 min
Serves 9

250g plain flour
50g polenta
1 tbsp caster sugar
1 tbsp baking powder
12 sunblush tomatoes, chopped
75g mozzarella, drained and
  chopped
250ml milk
2 large eggs
4 tbsp olive oil
4 tsp grated Parmesan cheese
18 cherry tomatoes, halved
1 tbsp fresh basil leaves (torn),
  plus 9 sprigs fresh basil,
  to serve

1. Preheat the oven to 375°F (190°C). Place paper cases in a 9-hole muffin tin.

2. Mix together the flour, polenta, sugar and baking powder in a mixing bowl. Add a generous pinch of salt and a pinch of pepper. Stir in the tomatoes, mozzarella and basil leaves.

3. Whisk together the milk, eggs and olive oil. Pour into the flour mixture and stir until just combined. The batter should remain lumpy.

4. Spoon the mixture into the paper cases. Sprinkle over the Parmesan cheese.

5. Place the cherry tomatoes in a greased roasting tin. Bake the tomatoes and muffins for 20 minutes until the muffins are well risen and firm and the tomatoes are tender.

6. Top the muffins with the roasted tomatoes and garnish with basil. Serve warm.

Bacon and onion muffins

1. Heat the oven to 400°F (200°C). Place paper cases in a 12-hole muffin tray.

2. Fry the bacon gently without the fat. Add the onions and fry briefly with the bacon. Drain on a kitchen paper. Reserve a little bacon for the garnish.

3. Mix the flour, baking powder, bicarbonate of soda and salt in a mixing bowl.

4. Whisk together the eggs, milk and soured cream in a separate bowl and add to the dry ingredients, whisking all the while. Add a little more milk if necessary. Stir in the bacon and onion.

5. Spoon into the paper cases and bake for about 25 minutes until golden and risen.

6. Garnish with a spoonful of soured cream, the reserved chopped bacon, chopped parsley and a pinch of ground pepper. Serve warm.

Preparation time: 15 min
Cooking time: 25 min
Serves 12

200g chopped bacon
1 onion, chopped
300g plain flour
3 tsp baking powder
½ tsp bicarbonate of soda
½ tsp salt
2 eggs
125ml soured cream
50ml milk
50ml soured cream, to serve
2 tbsp freshly chopped parsley,
* to serve*

Blueberry cupcakes

1. Preheat the oven to 400°F (200°C). Place paper cases in a 12-hole cupcake tray.

2. Sift the flour, cocoa, baking powder and cinnamon into a mixing bowl. Stir in the sugar.

3. Whisk together the eggs and oil in a separate bowl until frothy, then slowly whisk in the milk. Stir into the dry ingredients until just blended. Gently stir in the blueberries.

4. Spoon into the paper cases and bake for 20 minutes until risen and springy to the touch. Cool in the tins for 5 minutes, then place on a wire rack to cool completely.

5. For the topping: whisk the cream until thick and spoon into a piping bag. Pipe a swirl on top of each cake and decorate with silver baubles.

Preparation time: 15 min
Cooking time: 20 min
Serves 12

200g plain flour
25g cocoa powder
2 tsp baking powder
1 tsp ground cinnamon
110g caster sugar
2 eggs
100ml sunflower oil
225ml milk
110g blueberries

For the topping:
300ml double cream

To decorate:
edible silver baubles

Making chocolate meringues

Meringues are a versatile dessert option and make a great topping for muffins.

STEP 1 In a large, clean mixing bowl, whisk together the egg whites and cream of tartar until soft peaks form.

STEP 2 Gradually whisk in the sugar, adding it 1 tablespoon at a time, until the mixture is stiff and glossy.

STEP 3 Sift in the cocoa powder, if using, holding the sieve high to incorporate as much air as possible.

STEP 4 Using a large metal spoon, gently fold the cocoa powder into the egg whites, without expelling any air.

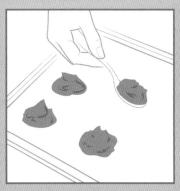

STEP 5 Line a baking sheet with greaseproof paper and spoon on the mixture. Bake according to the recipe.

Poppy seed cupcakes with sour cherries

1. Preheat the oven to 400°F (200°C). Grease a 12-hole muffin tray.

2. Mix together the flour, sugar, baking powder, bicarbonate of soda, salt and poppy seeds in a mixing bowl.

3. Whisk the buttermilk, butter and egg until smooth. Stir into the flour mixture, until just combined. Reserve 12 sour cherries and gently stir the remainder into the mixture.

4. Spoon into the tins. Place a sour cherry on top of each muffin and bake for about 20 minutes until golden and risen. Cool in the tray for 5 minutes, then place on a wire rack to cool completely.

Preparation time: 10 min
Cooking time: 20 min
Serves 12

200g plain flour
175g caster sugar
2 ½ tsp baking powder
½ tsp bicarbonate of soda
½ tsp salt
1 tbsp poppy seeds, lightly toasted
300ml buttermilk
2 tbsp butter, melted
1 large egg, whisked
140g dried sour cherries

Ricotta and raspberry muffins

1. Preheat the oven to 400°F (200°C). Grease a 12-hole muffin tray.

2. Mix together the egg and oil in a mixing bowl until blended. Stir in the ricotta.

3. Sift in the flour and baking powder and stir into the mixture with the sugar and salt until just combined. Gently stir in the raspberries.

4. Spoon into the tins and bake for about 20 minutes until risen and golden. Cool in the tray for a few minutes, then place on a wire rack to cool completely.

5. To decorate: push the raspberries through a sieve into a bowl and mix with the apple juice and sugar. Spoon the sauce over the muffins. Sift a little icing sugar over the top and place a raspberry on top of each muffin.

Preparation time: 15 min
Cooking time: 20 min
Serves 12

1 egg
75ml sunflower oil
150g ricotta
200g plain flour
2 tsp baking powder
100g caster sugar
1 pinch salt
150g frozen raspberries

To decorate:
250g raspberries
2 tbsp sugar
3 tbsp apple juice
icing sugar
12 fresh raspberries

Espressso cupcakes with mascarpone cream

1. Preheat the oven to 350°F (180°C). Place paper cases in a 12-hole cupcake tray.

2. Sift the flour and baking powder into a mixing bowl and stir in the sugar. Whisk in the eggs and coffee, beating well until combined.

3. Spoon into the paper cases and bake for about 20 minutes until risen and springy to the touch. Leave in the tray for 5 minutes then place on a wire rack to cool completely.

4. For the mascarpone cream: whisk the butter until soft, then sift in the icing sugar. Gradually whisk in the mascarpone until smooth and creamy. Spoon a little mascarpone cream on top of each cake and sprinkle with instant coffee.

Preparation time: 15 min
Cooking time: 20 min
Serves 12

110g self-raising flour
110g light brown sugar
110g butter, softened
2 eggs, whisked
1 tbsp cold strong black coffee

For the mascarpone cream:
175g butter
350g icing sugar
225g mascarpone

To decorate:
7–8 tsp instant coffee powder

Elegant chocolate muffin

Preparation time: 20 min
Cooking time: 30 min
Serves 12

150g honey
100g dark brown sugar
75g butter
3 tbsp milk
250g plain flour
2 tsp baking powder
2 tbsp cocoa powder
2 eggs, whisked

For the icing:
225g icing sugar
25g cocoa powder
25g sugar
3 tbsp water

To decorate:
sugar flowers

1. Preheat the oven to 325°F (160°C). Place paper cases in a 12-hole muffin tray.

2. Warm the honey, sugar, butter and milk in a pan until the sugar dissolves. Stir and allow to cool.

3. Sift the flour, baking powder and cocoa into a mixing bowl. Stir in the cooled honey mixture until blended, then stir in the eggs until smooth.

4. Spoon into the paper cases and bake for 25 minutes. Leave in the tins for 5 minutes then place on a wire rack to cool completely.

5. For the icing: sift the icing sugar into a bowl. Heat the cocoa, sugar and water in a pan over a low heat until the sugar has dissolved. Bring to the boil then immediately remove from the heat. Pour onto the icing sugar and beat until smooth. Use while warm as this icing sets quickly.

6. Spread the icing on top of the muffins and decorate with sugar flowers.

Cupcake with buttercream and blackberries

1. Preheat the oven to 350°F (180°C). Place paper cases in a 12-hole cupcake tray.

2. Mix the flour and sugar together in a mixing bowl.

3. Whisk the eggs with the yoghurt, then pour into the dry ingredients with the melted butter and lemon zest. Mix together until just combined.

4. Spoon into the paper cases and bake for 20–25 minutes until risen and firm to the touch. Cool for 5 minutes in the tins, then place on a wire rack to cool completely.

5. For the buttercream: whisk the butter until soft and creamy. Mix in the cream and vanilla until blended. Sift in the icing sugar and beat until smooth. Spoon into a piping bag and pipe a generous swirl on top of each cake.

6. To decorate: chop the blackberries and scatter over the cream. Place a whole blackberry on top of each swirl of cream.

Preparation time: 20 min
Cooking time: 25 min
Serves 12

225g self-raising flour
175g caster sugar
3 eggs
100ml plain yoghurt
175g butter, melted
1 lemon, finely grated zest

For the buttercream:
50g unsalted butter
100ml double cream
½ tsp vanilla extract
350g icing sugar

To decorate:
110g blackberries
12 whole blackberries

Cupcake with buttercream and raspberries

1. Preheat the oven to 400°F (200°C). Place paper cases in a 12-hole cupcake tray.

2. Mix the flour with the almonds, baking powder and bicarbonate of soda.

3. Whisk the egg lightly in a mixing bowl. Add the sugar, oil, orange juice and buttermilk and mix well. Quickly stir the flour mixture into the egg mixture.

4. Spoon into the paper cases and bake for 25–30 minutes until golden and risen. Cool in the tray for 5 minutes, then place on a wire rack to cool completely.

5. For the buttercream: whisk the butter until soft. Gradually sift in the icing sugar and stir until smooth. Whisk in the custard.

6. Spoon the mixture into a piping bag and pipe on top of the cakes. Sprinkle with sugar pearls and place a raspberry on each whirl of buttercream. Sift a little icing sugar over the cakes. Chill until ready to serve.

Preparation time: 20 min
Cooking time: 30 min
Serves 12

250g plain flour
50g ground almonds
2 tsp baking powder
½ tsp bicarbonate of soda
1 egg
100g caster sugar
80ml vegetable oil
150ml orange juice
120ml buttermilk

For the buttercream:
150g butter
3 tbsp icing sugar
3 tbsp thick custard

To decorate:
12 raspberries
icing sugar
sugar pearls

Carrot cupcakes

1. Preheat the oven to 350°F (180°C). Place 15 paper cases in cupcake trays.

2. Place the eggs, sugar and oil in a large bowl and whisk with an electric whisk for 2–3 minutes until light and fluffy. Gently fold in the flour, spices, grated carrot, vanilla extract and the orange zest, until thoroughly combined.

3. Spoon into the paper cases and bake for 20–25 minutes until well risen and golden brown. Place on a wire rack to cool completely.

4. For the cream icing: whisk the cream, icing sugar and vanilla with the hot water until thick, smooth and spreadable.

5. Spread the icing on top of each cake and decorate with edible flowers.

Preparation time: 15 min
Cooking time: 25 min
Serves 15

2 eggs
175g caster sugar
150ml sunflower oil
200g self-raising flour
2 tsp mixed spice
1 tsp ground cinnamon
2 carrots, coarsely grated
1 tsp vanilla extract
1 orange, finely grated zest

For the cream icing:
50g double cream
225g icing sugar, sifted
2 tsp vanilla extract
2–3 tbsp very hot water

To decorate:
edible flowers, e.g. borage,
cornflowers, etc.

Fig muffins

Preparation time: 10 min
Cooking time: 30 min
Serves 12

300g self-raising flour
1 tsp baking powder
2 tsp ground cinnamon
pinch salt
100g caster sugar
250ml milk
2 eggs, whisked
100g butter, melted
150g chopped figs
100g chopped hazelnuts
100g whole hazelnuts

1. Preheat the oven to 400°F (200°C). Grease a 12-hole muffin tray.

2. Mix the flour, baking powder, cinnamon and salt together in a mixing bowl, then stir in the sugar.

3. Mix the milk, eggs and melted butter in a large jug and pour into the dry ingredients. Stir until just combined. The mixture will be lumpy.

4. Spoon the mixture into the tins to half-fill them. Place the figs on top and cover with more mixture. Sprinkle with chopped and whole hazelnuts.

5. Bake for 25–30 minutes until the muffins are risen and golden. Cool in the tray for a few minutes, then place on a wire rack to cool completely.

Chocolate mint cupcakes

1. Preheat the oven to 350°F (180°C). Grease a 12-hole cupcake tray.

2. Whisk the butter and sugar in a mixing bowl until soft and creamy. Mix in the eggs and milk.

3. Sift in the flour, salt, bicarbonate of soda and cocoa and stir well to mix.

4. Spoon the mixture into the tray. Bake for about 15 minutes, until a skewer inserted into the centre of one of the cupcakes comes out clean. Remove from the tray and place on a wire rack to cool completely.

5. For the mint buttercream: whisk the butter in a bowl until soft. Sift in the icing sugar and whisk until smooth. Mix in the cream and peppermint until blended. Stir in a few drops of green food colouring.

6. Spoon into a piping bag and pipe on top of the cupcakes. Chill before serving.

Preparation time: 20 mins
  plus chilling
Cooking time: 15 min
Serves 12

150g butter
300g caster sugar
3 eggs, beaten
250ml milk
225g plain flour
pinch salt
1 tsp bicarbonate of soda
50g cocoa powder
75g chocolate chips

For the mint buttercream:
100g unsalted butter
200g icing sugar
1–2 tbsp double cream
3–4 drops peppermint extract
green food colouring

Valentine's day cupcakes

1. Preheat the oven to 350°F (180°C). Place paper cases in 2 x 12-hole mini muffin trays.

2. Mix the prunes with the apple juice in a bowl and knead by hand until they have absorbed the liquid.

3. Whisk together the egg yolks, butter, 40g sugar, salt and vanilla until smooth. Stir in the chocolate and milk, followed by the prunes.

4. Whisk the egg whites with the remaining sugar until stiff. Gently fold into the mixture. Sift in the flour and baking powder and stir in until just combined.

5. Spoon into the paper cases and bake for 12–15 minutes until risen. Cool in the trays for 5 minutes, then place on a wire rack to cool completely.

6. For the marzipan hearts: knead the marzipan until softened. Knead in a few drops of red food colouring. Roll out on a work surface sprinkled with icing sugar and cut out small heart shapes.

7. Whisk the cream until stiff and stir in 1 or 2 drops of red food colouring to tint it pink.

8. Spread the cream on top of the cakes and decorate with marzipan hearts and sugar pearls.

Preparation time: 25 min
Cooking time: 15 min
Serves 24

100g prunes, chopped
50ml apple juice
2 eggs, separated
50g butter, softened
90g caster sugar
pinch salt
1 tsp vanilla extract
125g plain chocolate, melted
125ml milk
120g plain flour
1 tsp baking powder

For the marzipan hearts:
110g marzipan
Red food colouring
150ml double cream

To decorate:
icing sugar
small sugar pearls

Chocolate and coconut cupcakes

1. Preheat the oven to 400°F (200°C). Place paper cases in a 12-hole cupcake tray.

2. Mix the mascarpone, vanilla and half the sugar until smooth and chill.

3. Whisk the egg whites with the salt until stiff.

4. Whisk the egg yolks with the remaining sugar in a mixing bowl until thick and creamy. Sift in the espresso powder, flour, cornflour and baking powder and fold in thoroughly.

5. Stir the melted chocolate into the mascarpone. Pour the mascarpone mixture into the flour mixture and mix thoroughly.

6. Fold the whisked egg whites into the mixture until blended.

7. Spoon into the paper cases and bake for 20–25 minutes until risen. Cool in the tray for a few minutes then place on a wire rack to cool completely.

8. For the topping: heat the cream, add the white chocolate, stir until dissolved and chill until thickened.

9. Whisk the chocolate topping until creamy. Spoon into a piping bag and pipe onto the cupcakes. Decorate with shredded coconut. Chill until ready to serve.

Preparation time: 20 mins
  plus 1 h chilling
Cooking time: 25 min
Serves 12

200g mascarpone
1 tsp vanilla extract
150g caster sugar
3 eggs, separated
pinch of salt
1 tbsp instant espresso powder
100g plain flour
50g cornflour
2 tsp baking powder
200g plain chocolate, 70% cocoa, melted

For the topping:
100ml double cream
50g good-quality white chocolate, chopped
50g shredded coconut, toasted

Valentine's day cupcakes with candy hearts

1. Preheat the oven to 350°F (180°C). Place paper cases in a 12-hole cupcake tray.

2. Melt the chocolate in a heatproof bowl over a pan of simmering (not boiling) water.

3. Whisk the flour, sugar, cocoa, oil, soured cream, eggs, vanilla and water until smooth. Whisk in the melted chocolate.

4. Spoon into the paper cases and bake for 20 minutes until a skewer inserted comes out clean. Remove from the tray and cool on a wire rack.

5. For the topping: whisk the butter until very soft. Sift in the icing sugar and beat until smooth. Divide the buttercream into 3 and put 2 portions into 2 small bowls.

6. Stir the vanilla extract into one-third; the melted chocolate into another third and the lemon juice and yellow colouring into the remaining third.

7. Spread the buttercream over the top of each cake and decorate with candy hearts.

Preparation time: 15 min
Cooking time: 20 min
Serves 12

*100g semi-sweet chocolate,
    50% cocoa solids, chopped*
200g self-raising flour
225g light brown sugar
6 tbsp cocoa powder
150ml sunflower oil
100ml soured cream
2 eggs
1 tsp vanilla extract
100ml warm water

For the topping:
150g unsalted butter
350g icing sugar
few drops vanilla extract
25g plain chocolate, melted
2 tsp lemon juice
yellow food colouring

To decorate:
candy hearts

Sausage and cheese muffin

1. Preheat the oven to 400°F (200°C). Grease a 10-hole muffin tray.

2. Combine the flour, courgettes, salt, pepper and cheese in a mixing bowl and mix well.

3. Mix together the milk, egg and oil. Stir into the dry ingredients and mix well. Stir in the sausage.

4. Spoon into the tins and sprinkle with grated cheddar.

5. Bake for about 20 minutes until golden brown and the cheese is bubbling. Serve immediately.

Preparation time: 10 min
Cooking time: 20 min
Serves 10

225g self-raising flour
100g grated courgettes
100g grated Cheddar
175ml milk
1 egg
55ml sunflower oil
4–5 cooked sausages, diced
salt and pepper, to taste

For the topping:
100g grated Cheddar

Southwestern corn muffin with chicken

Preparation time: 20 min
Cooking time: 40 min
Serves 12

1 tbsp oil
1 sweetcorn cob, kernels
  sliced off
3 spring onions, finely chopped
150g plain flour
150g polenta
2 tsp baking powder
1 tsp salt
50g grated Cheddar
2 eggs
285ml buttermilk
100ml milk
85g butter, melted
3 firm tomatoes, chopped
225g coarsely chopped cooked
  chicken

1. Preheat the oven to 400°F (200°C). Grease a 12-hole muffin tray.

2. Heat the oil in a pan and cook the corn kernels and spring onions for 5–10 minutes until golden and soft.

3. Mix together the flour, polenta, baking powder, salt and cheese in a mixing bowl.

4. Whisk together the eggs, buttermilk and milk, then stir into the dry ingredients with the melted butter and corn mixture. Stir in the tomatoes.

5. Half-fill the tray with the mixture. Place a layer of chicken on top and cover with more mixture to fill the holes.

6. Bake for 25–30 minutes until golden and risen. Serve warm.

Cherry almond muffins

1. Preheat the oven to 350°F (180°C). Place large squares of greaseproof paper in a 12-hole muffin tray.

2. Mix the sugar, vanilla, egg, butter and yoghurt together.

3. Sift the flour and baking powder into a mixing bowl. Add the almonds. Stir in the egg mixture and mix quickly. The mixture will be lumpy. Stir in the cherries.

4. Spoon into the lined tray and place flaked almonds on top of each muffin.

5. Bake for 20 minutes until risen and golden. Place on a wire rack to cool completely.

Preparation time: 15 min
Cooking time: 20 min
Serves 12

150g caster sugar
1 tsp vanilla extract
1 egg
125g butter, melted
175ml plain yoghurt
200g plain flour
1 tsp baking powder
100g ground almonds
225g glacé cherries, halved
75g flaked almonds

Cupcake with ice cream layers and chocolate frosting

1. Preheat the oven to 350°F (180°C). Place paper cases in a 12-hole cupcake tray.

2. Whisk the butter and sugar in a mixing bowl until light and fluffy. Stir in the vanilla.

3. Sift in the flour, salt and cornflour and lightly fold into the mixture, alternating with the eggs until well blended.

4. Spoon into the paper cases and bake for about 20–25 minutes until golden and springy to the touch.

5. Cool in the tray for 5 minutes, then place on a wire rack to cool completely.

6. Split each cupcake into three, using a sharp knife. Place half a scoop of strawberry ice cream on one layer and spread quickly over the cake. Top with a layer of cupcake. Spread with another half scoop of strawberry ice cream and top with the third layer of cake. Place the cakes in the freezer.

7. For the chocolate topping: whisk the butter until soft and sift in the cocoa powder. Stir well, then sift in the icing sugar and vanilla. Mix well.

8. Spread the topping over the top of each cake. The cakes can be placed in the freezer as you work. Sprinkle with sugar crystals just before serving.

Preparation time: 20 min
Cooking time: 25 min
Serves 12

110g butter
110g caster sugar
1 tsp vanilla extract
110g self-raising flour
pinch of salt
1 tsp cornflour
2 eggs, whisked

For the ice cream filling:
12 scoops strawberry ice cream

For the chocolate topping:
50g butter
20g cocoa powder
75g icing sugar
1 tsp vanilla extract

To decorate:
sugar crystals

Dried apricot, cranberry and walnut cupcakes

1. Preheat the oven to 350°F (180°C). Place paper cases in a 12-hole deep cupcake or muffin tray.

2. Whisk the butter and sugar together until light and fluffy. Gradually whisk in the eggs until blended.

3. Sift in the flour and beat well. Stir in the vanilla and cream.

4. Spoon into the paper cases and bake for 20–25 minutes until golden and risen. Cool in the tray for 5 minutes then place on a wire rack to cool.

5. For the icing: sift the icing sugar into a bowl and gradually stir in the lemon juice and water until the mixture is smooth and thick. Spread a thick layer of icing on top of each cake.

6. Scatter the apricots, walnuts and cranberries over the top of each cake before the icing sets.

Preparation time: 20 min
Cooking time: 25 min
Serves 12

225g butter
225g caster sugar
4 eggs, beaten
225g self-raising flour
1 tsp vanilla essence
1 tbsp double cream

For the icing:
350g icing sugar
3 tbsp lemon juice
1–2 tsp water

For the topping:
150g ready to eat dried apricots,
*   chopped*
120g chopped walnuts
110g dried cranberries

Chocolate marshmallow walnut cupcakes

Preparation time: 25 min
Cooking time: 15 min
Serves 12

150g butter
300g caster sugar
3 eggs, whisked
250ml milk
225g plain flour
pinch of salt
1 tsp bicarbonate of soda
50g cocoa powder

For the chocolate frosting:
110g dark chocolate, 60% cocoa
  solids
150g butter
160g icing sugar, sifted
1 tsp vanilla extract

For the decoration:
110g dark chocolate, roughly
  chopped
110g chopped walnuts
mini marshmallows

1. Preheat the oven to 350°F (180°C). Place paper cases in a 12-hole cupcake tray.

2. Whisk the butter and sugar in a mixing bowl until soft and creamy. Mix in the eggs and milk.

3. Sift in the flour, salt, bicarbonate of soda and cocoa and stir well to mix.

4. Spoon the mixture into the paper cases. Bake for about 15 minutes, until a skewer inserted into the centre comes out clean. Remove from the tray and place on a wire rack to cool completely.

5. For the chocolate frosting: melt the chocolate in a heatproof bowl over a pan of simmering (not boiling) water. Remove from the heat and cool to room temperature.

6. Whisk the butter with an electric whisk until smooth and creamy. Add the sugar and mix until light and fluffy. Mix in the vanilla and melted chocolate and whisk on low speed until incorporated. Increase the speed and whisk until the mixture is smooth and glossy.

7. Spread the frosting on the cakes and decorate with chopped chocolate, walnuts and mini marshmallows.

Light lemon cupcakes

1. Preheat the oven to 350°F (180°C). Place paper cases in a 12-hole cupcake tray.

2. Whisk the butter and sugar in a mixing bowl until pale and fluffy. Gradually mix in the eggs until blended. Fold in the flour, salt and lemon zest until blended.

3. Spoon the mixture into the paper cases and bake for 15–20 minutes, until golden brown and springy to the touch. Place on a wire rack to cool completely.

4. For the buttercream: whisk the butter until soft and creamy. Mix in the cream and vanilla until blended.

5. Sift in the icing sugar and beat until smooth. Spoon into a piping bag and pipe on top of the cakes.

6. Scatter the sprinkles and sparkling sugar over the buttercream just before serving.

Preparation time: 20 min
Cooking time: 20 min
Serves 12

110g butter
110g caster sugar
2 eggs, whisked
110g self-raising flour
pinch of salt
1 lemon, finely grated zest

For the buttercream:
50g unsalted butter
100ml double cream
½ tsp vanilla extract
350g icing sugar

To decorate:
yellow sugar sprinkles
yellow sparkling sugar

Chocolate cupcake with pink buttercream frosting

1. Preheat the oven to 375°F (190°C). Place paper cases in a 12-hole cupcake tray.

2. Place all the ingredients in a mixing bowl and whisk with an electric whisk until blended. Alternatively, beat well with a wooden spoon.

3. Spoon the mixture into the paper cases and bake for 20–25 minutes until golden and springy to the touch. Remove from the tray and place on a wire rack to cool completely.

4. For the buttercream: whisk the butter in a bowl until soft. Sift in the icing sugar and beat well. Stir in the pink food colouring and rosewater.

5. Spoon into a piping bag. Pipe swirls on each cake. Scatter with sugar sprinkles.

Preparation time: 20 min
Cooking time: 25 min
Serves 12

150g butter, softened
150g caster sugar
175g self-raising flour
3 eggs, whisked
2 tbsp cocoa powder

For the buttercream:
120g unsalted butter
200g icing sugar
few drops pink food colouring
½ tsp rosewater

For the decoration:
white sugar sprinkles

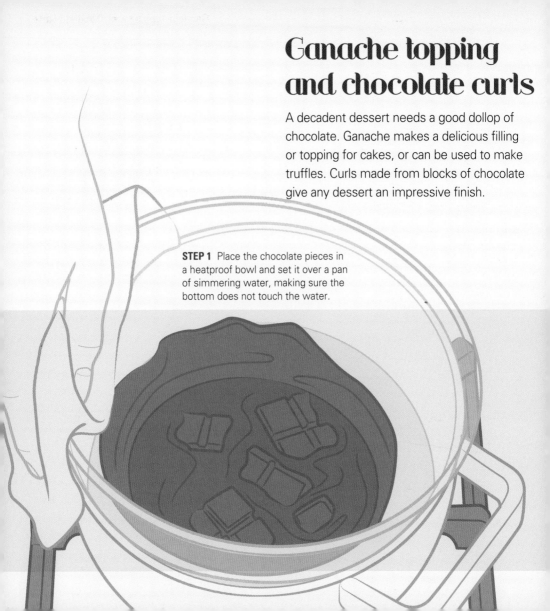

Ganache topping and chocolate curls

A decadent dessert needs a good dollop of chocolate. Ganache makes a delicious filling or topping for cakes, or can be used to make truffles. Curls made from blocks of chocolate give any dessert an impressive finish.

STEP 1 Place the chocolate pieces in a heatproof bowl and set it over a pan of simmering water, making sure the bottom does not touch the water.

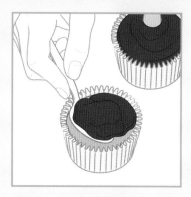

STEP 2 For the ganache, bring the cream to a boil in a saucepan and pour it over the chocolate in a large bowl. Stir to combine until smooth.

STEP 3 Once completely combined, set aside the ganache to cool, then chill for 1 hour. Use the thickened icing to top cooled cupcakes.

STEP 4 For curls, pour melted chocolate onto a chilled plate and set aside in the fridge until hard.

STEP 5 Once hard, push a knife over the flat chocolate surface to create curls or small shards.

Meringue cupcakes

1. Preheat the oven to 350°F (180°C). Place paper cases in a 12-hole cupcake tray.

2. Whisk the butter and sugar in a mixing bowl until soft and creamy. Gradually mix in the eggs until smooth.

3. Sift in the flour and baking powder and gently stir into the mixture with the lemon zest and juice until blended. Spoon into the paper cases.

4. For the meringue: whisk the egg whites until they stand in soft peaks. Gradually whisk in the sugar until the mixture is stiff.

5. Spoon on top of the cakes, swirling the mixture into peaks. Bake for 20–25 minutes until the meringue is crisp and browned and the cakes are cooked. Place on a wire rack to cool completely before serving.

Preparation time: 20 min
Cooking time: 25 min
Serves 12

110g unsalted butter
110g caster sugar
2 eggs
110g self-raising flour
1 tsp baking powder
1 lemon, finely grated zest
2 tbsp lemon juice

For the meringue:
2 egg whites
100g caster sugar

Frosted coffee cupcake

1. Preheat the oven to 350°F (180°C). Place paper cases in a 12-hole cupcake tray.

2. Whisk together the butter, sugar, flour, salt and eggs with 4 teaspoons of the coffee and a pinch of salt until creamy.

3. Spoon the mixture into the paper cases and bake for about 20 minutes until springy to the touch. Remove to a wire rack to cool completely.

4. For the coffee buttercream: whisk the butter until soft. Sift in the icing sugar and beat until light and fluffy. Beat in the remaining coffee until smooth. If the mixture is too stiff, add a little hot water.

5. Spoon into a piping bag and pipe a swirl on each cake. Chill until ready to serve.

Preparation time: 15 min
Cooking time: 20 min
Serves 12

110g butter
110g light brown sugar
110g self-raising flour
pinch of salt
2 large eggs
3 tsp instant espresso coffee
  powder, dissolved in 100ml
  boiling water

For the coffee buttercream:
100g butter
225g icing sugar
hot water

Peanut butter frosted chocolate cupcake

1. Preheat the oven to 350°F (180°C). Place paper cases in a 12-hole cupcake tray.

2. Whisk the butter and sugar in a mixing bowl until light and soft. Gradually whisk in the egg and vanilla then stir in the melted chocolate.

3. Sift in the flour and bicarbonate of soda and stir into the mixture alternately with the hot water until the mixture is smooth.

4. Pour into the paper cases and bake for 25–30 minutes until risen and firm to the touch.

5. Cool in the tray for 5 minutes, then place on a wire rack to cool completely.

6. For the frosting: whisk the butter and peanut butter with an electric whisk until smooth. Add the icing sugar and salt and mix until blended. Mix in the vanilla and cream and continue mixing until light and fluffy.

7. Spoon into a piping bag and pipe a swirl on top of each cake. Decorate with the sweets.

Preparation time: 20 min
Cooking time: 30 min
Serves 12

110g butter
200g dark brown sugar
1 egg, whisked
½ tsp vanilla extract
75g plain chocolate chips, melted
110g plain flour
½ tsp bicarbonate of soda
125ml hot water

For the peanut butter frosting:
8 tbsp unsalted butter
110g smooth peanut butter
75g icing sugar
pinch of salt
½ tsp vanilla extract
1 tbsp double cream

To decorate:
chocolate coated peanut sweets

Orange zest muffins

Preparation time: 15 min
Cooking time: 25 min
Serves 10

75g butter, melted
1 egg, whisked
175ml plain yoghurt
1 orange, juice and finely
  grated zest
250g plain flour
1 tbsp baking powder
150g sugar

To decorate:
1 large orange, coarsely
  grated zest

1. Preheat the oven to 350°F (180°C). Place paper cases in a 10-hole muffin tray.

2. Combine the butter, egg, yoghurt, orange juice and zest in a mixing bowl. Sift in the flour, baking powder and sugar.

3. Spoon the mixture into the paper cases and bake for 25 minutes until golden and risen. Leave in the tray for 5 minutes, then place on a wire rack to cool completely.

4. Place a little orange zest on each muffin.

Chocolate muffin with cream filling

1. Preheat the oven to 400°F (200°C). Grease a 12-hole muffin tray.

2. Melt the chocolate and butter in a heatproof bowl over a pan of simmering (not boiling) water. Remove from the heat and stir once.

3. Sift the flour, baking powder and cocoa into a mixing bowl. Stir in the sugar.

4. Mix the egg and milk together and slowly stir into the melted chocolate. Stir the mixture into the dry ingredients until only just combined.

5. Spoon into the tins and scatter a few hazelnuts over the top of each muffin.

6. Bake for 20–25 minutes until well risen and firm. Leave to cool in the tray for 5 minutes then place on a wire rack to cool completely.

7. Split each muffin in half. Whisk the cream until thick and spoon into a piping bag. Pipe a swirl of cream on 12 muffin halves. Replace the tops and sift over a little icing sugar.

Preparation time: 20 min
Cooking time: 25 min
Serves 12

175g dark chocolate chips
50g butter
375g self-raising flour
1 tbsp baking powder
4 tbsp cocoa powder
100g caster sugar
350ml milk
75g chopped hazelnuts

For the filling:
300ml double cream

To decorate:
icing sugar

Moist peach muffins

1. Preheat the oven to 400°F (200°C). Place paper cases in a 6-hole muffin tray.

2. Whisk together the flour, eggs, milk and sugar in a mixing bowl until smooth.

3. Pour into the paper cases. Top each muffin with a peach half, pressing them down into the mixture.

4. Bake in the oven for about 10 minutes until golden. Place on a wire rack to cool completely.

Preparation time: 15 min
Cooking time: 10 min
Serves 6

110g self-raising flour
2 eggs
100ml milk
2 tbsp caster sugar
6 canned peach halves

Chocolate muffin with Nutella filling

1. Preheat the oven to 400°F (200°C). Grease a 12-hole muffin tray.

2. Sift the flour, cocoa and baking powder into a mixing bowl. Stir in the sugar.

3. Whisk together the eggs and oil in a separate bowl until frothy, then slowly whisk in the milk. Stir into the dry ingredients until just blended. Stir in the chocolate chips.

4. Spoon into the tray to half-fill the holes. Place about 2 teaspoons of Nutella on top of each muffin, then cover with the rest of the muffin mixture. Bake for 15–20 minutes until risen and springy to the touch. Cool in the tray for 5 minutes then place on a wire rack to cool completely.

5. For the chocolate ganache: bring the cream to a boil in a pan. Remove from the heat and stir in the chocolate until melted. Stir in the butter, stirring until the mixture is glossy. Chill for about 1 hour until thick.

6. Whisk the ganache with an electric whisk until increased in volume and thick. Spoon the ganache into a piping bag and pipe on top of the muffins. Place a cherry half on top of the ganache.

Preparation time: 15 min
plus 1 h chilling
Cooking time: 20 min
Serves 9

200g plain flour
25g cocoa powder
1 tbsp baking powder
110g light brown sugar
2 eggs
100ml sunflower oil
225ml milk
75g chocolate chips
8 tbsp Nutella

For the chocolate ganache:
175ml double cream
175g chopped dark chocolate
25g butter

To decorate:
6 cherries, pitted and halved

Apricot muffin

Preparation time: 15 min
Cooking time: 15 min
Serves 8

3 egg whites
125g icing sugar
40g plain flour
100g ground almonds
100g unsalted butter, melted
½ tsp vanilla extract
3 ripe apricots, skinned, pitted
  and diced

1. Preheat the oven to 400°F (200°C). Grease an 8-hole muffin tray.

2. Whisk the egg whites until soft peaks form.

3. Place the dry ingredients into a mixing bowl. Gently stir in the egg whites, melted butter and vanilla until combined. Gently stir in the apricots.

4. Spoon into the tray and bake for 10–15 minutes until risen and golden. Cool in the tray for a few minutes, then place on a wire rack to cool completely.

Banana muffins

1. Preheat the oven to 375°F (190°C). Place paper cases in a 10-hole muffin tray.

2. Sift the flour, baking powder, bicarbonate of soda, salt, cinnamon and nutmeg together in a bowl. Stir in the sugar.

3. Whisk the eggs, vanilla, oil and milk in a mixing bowl. Mash the bananas with a fork and stir into the mixture. Make a well in the centre of the dry ingredients and add the egg mixture, stirring until just combined. The mixture will be lumpy.

4. Spoon into the paper cases and bake for 20–25 minutes until the muffins are risen and golden. Cool in the tray for 5 minutes, then place on a wire rack to cool completely.

Preparation time: 15 min
Cooking time: 25 min
Serves 10

250g self-raising flour
1 tsp baking powder
½ tsp bicarbonate of soda
pinch salt
½ tsp ground cinnamon
½ tsp grated nutmeg
110g caster sugar
2 eggs
1 tsp vanilla extract
75ml sunflower oil
125ml milk
2 large, very ripe bananas

Passion fruit and blueberry cupcakes

1. Preheat the oven to 350°F (180°C). Grease a 12-hole cupcake tray.

2. Whisk the butter, sugar and vanilla in a mixing bowl, until light and creamy. Add the eggs, one at a time and mix well after each addition. Add the mascarpone and the passion fruit pulp (including the pips) and mix until smooth.

3. Stir in both flours alternately with the milk until smooth.

4. Spoon into the tins and bake for 20 minutes until golden and springy to the touch. Cool in the tray for 5 minutes, then place on a wire rack to cool completely.

5. For the passion fruit cream: whisk the mascarpone, cream and icing sugar in a bowl until blended and beginning to thicken. Stir in the passion fruit pulp and mix until firm.

6. Spoon on top of each cake. Place a bluberry on top of each cake and sift over a little icing sugar.

Preparation time: 20 min
Cooking time: 20 min
Serves 12

185g unsalted butter
175g caster sugar
1 tsp vanilla extract
3 eggs
125g mascarpone
60ml passionfruit pulp
125g self-raising flour
30g plain flour
60ml milk

For the passion fruit cream:
250g mascarpone
50ml double cream
3 tbsp icing sugar
3 passion fruit, halved and pulp
   removed

To decorate:
12 blueberries
icing sugar

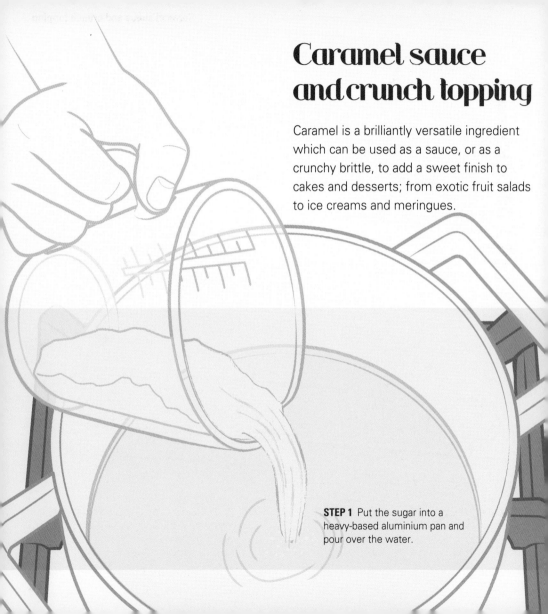

Caramel sauce and crunch topping

Caramel is a brilliantly versatile ingredient which can be used as a sauce, or as a crunchy brittle, to add a sweet finish to cakes and desserts; from exotic fruit salads to ice creams and meringues.

STEP 1 Put the sugar into a heavy-based aluminium pan and pour over the water.

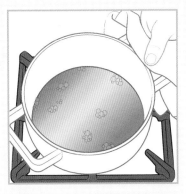

STEP 2 Heat gently, tilting the pan and not stirring, until the sugar has dissolved. Increase the heat and bubble for 4–5 minutes until golden brown.

STEP 3 For caramel sauce, remove the pan from the heat and carefully stir in the cream and the butter. Pour into a jug and leave to cool until needed.

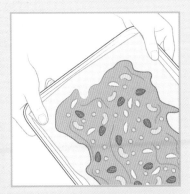

STEP 4 To make crunch topping, pour the caramel onto a lightly oiled baking tray and tilt it to spread evenly. For praline, first add nuts to the caramel.

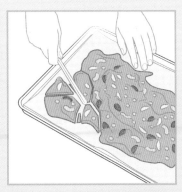

STEP 5 Set the mixture aside until completely cold and the caramel has set hard. Using a spatula, lift off the caramel, breaking it up as you go.

Blueberry muffins

1. Preheat the oven to 350°F (180°C). Place paper cases in a 12-hole muffin tray.

2. Toss the blueberries in 2 tablespoons of the flour. Set aside.

3. Mix the butter and sugar together in a mixing bowl until light and fluffy. Whisk in the egg.

4. Sift in the flour, baking powder, bicarbonate of soda and salt and stir until just combined. Gently stir in the yoghurt and blueberries.

5. Spoon into the paper cases and bake for 20 minutes until the muffins are golden and springy to the touch. Place on a wire rack to cool completely.

Preparation time: 15 min
Cooking time: 20 min
Serves 12

200g blueberries
250g plain flour
120g butter
175g caster sugar
1 egg
2½ tsp baking powder
½ tsp bicarbonate of soda
pinch salt
300ml plain yoghurt

Elegant raspberry muffins

1. Preheat the oven to 400°F (200°C). Place paper cases in a 10-hole muffin tray.

2. Sift the flour and baking powder together into a mixing bowl. Add the sugar.

3. Whisk together the butter, eggs and milk. Pour into the dry ingredients and stir until just combined. Stir in the raspberries.

4. Spoon the mixture into the paper cases and bake for 15–20 minutes until golden. Cool in the tray for a few minutes, then place on a wire rack to cool completely.

5. Place 3 raspberries on top of each muffin. Sift over the icing sugar.

Preparation time: 15 min
Cooking time: 20 min
Serves 10

300g plain flour
1 tbsp baking powder
100g caster sugar
100g unsalted butter, melted
2 large eggs
200ml milk
150g fresh raspberries

To decorate:
36 fresh raspberries
icing sugar

Papaya muffins

1. Preheat the oven to 400°F (200°C). Grease a 9-hole muffin tray.

2. Sift the plain flour into a mixing bowl and add the wholemeal flour, baking powder, bicarbonate of soda, papaya and sugar.

3. Mix together the oil, egg and milk and pour into the dry ingredients. Gently stir until just combined.

4. Spoon the mixture into the tray. Bake for 15 minutes until the muffins are risen and firm. Best served warm.

Preparation time: 15 min
Cooking time: 15 min
Serves 9

100g plain flour
125g wholemeal flour
2 tsp baking powder
pinch bicarbonate of soda
50g dried papaya, chopped
75g light brown sugar
100ml sunflower oil
1 egg
150ml milk

Black forest muffins

Preparation time: 15 min
Cooking time: 25 min
Serves 10

150g butter
110g light brown sugar
1 tsp vanilla extract
2 eggs, whisked
200g plain flour
25g cocoa powder
2 tsp baking powder
8 tbsp milk
50g dark chocolate, 60% cocoa
  solids, finely chopped

For the topping:
6 tbsp kirsch
300ml double cream
12 tbsp cherry jam
icing sugar

1. Preheat the oven to 350°F (180°C). Grease a 10-hole muffin tray.

2. Whisk the butter with an electric whisk until smooth. Gradually beat in the sugar and vanilla until very creamy.

3. Gradually mix in the eggs until blended.

4. Sift in the flour, cocoa and baking powder alternately with the milk and fold in gently until combined. Stir in the chocolate.

5. Spoon into the tray and bake for about 25 minutes until risen and firm to the touch. Cool in the tray for 5 minutes, then place on a wire rack to cool completely.

6. Slice the top off each muffin and sprinkle the muffin with kirsch. Whisk the cream until thick and lightly stir in the cherry jam, to give a marbled effect. Spoon the filling on each muffin and replace the tops.

7. Sift over a little icing sugar just before serving.

Courgette, feta and mint muffins

1. Preheat the oven to 375°F (190°C). Line a muffin tray with 12 paper muffin cases.

2. In a large bowl, sift together the flour and baking powder. Stir in the sugar and salt and pepper. Add the grated cheese and feta, reserving a little to sprinkle over the top, courgette and mint. Mix well with a metal spoon to combine all the ingredients.

3. In a jug, whisk together the eggs, milk and butter with a fork. Pour over the dry ingredients and stir until just combined. The batter should be lumpy.

4. Spoon the mixture between the muffin cases and sprinkle with the remaining cheese.

5. Bake in the centre of the oven for 20–25 minutes until risen, golden and firm. Can be served warm or cold.

Preparation time: 10 min
Cooking time: 25 min
Serves 12

275g plain flour
1 tbsp baking powder
1 tbsp caster sugar
1 tsp salt
½ tsp ground black pepper
50g mature Cheddar cheese, grated
125g feta, crumbled
2 medium-sized courgettes, grated
2 tbsp freshly chopped mint
2 medium eggs, whisked
175ml milk
75g lightly salted butter, melted

Fruity oat and honey breakfast muffins

1. Preheat the oven to 375°F (190°C). Line a muffin tray with 10 paper muffin cases.

2. In a large bowl, sift together the flour and baking powder. Using a metal spoon, stir in the oats, apricots, cranberries, seeds, sugar and salt.

3. In a jug, whisk together the eggs, milk, oil and honey, with a fork. Pour over the dry ingredients and stir until just combined, the batter should be lumpy and fairly runny.

4. Spoon the mixture between the muffin cases, so they are two-thirds full and cook on the top shelf of the oven for 20–25 minutes until risen and golden. Leave in the tray for a few minutes, then transfer to a wire rack to cool completely.

Preparation time: 10 min
Cooking time: 25 min
Serves 10

250g plain flour
1 tbsp baking powder
100g porridge oats
125g ready-to-eat dried apricots, chopped
50g dried cranberries
2 tbsp mixed seeds, e.g. sunflower, linseed, pumpkin, hemp
50g light soft brown sugar
½ tsp salt
2 medium eggs, whisked
175ml milk
75ml sunflower oil
4 tbsp clear honey

Elegant lemon cupcakes

1. Line 2 x 12-hole cupcake trays with 20 paper cases. Preheat the oven to 350°F (180°C).

2. Place the butter, sugar, flour, eggs and lemon extract in a bowl and whisk with a wooden spoon or electric whisk until pale and creamy.

3. Divide the mixture between the paper cases and level the tops. Bake for 15 minutes until golden and just firm. Cool in the tin for 5 minutes, then transfer to a wire rack to cool completely. Trim any pointed tops to make a flat surface.

4. Place the icing sugar in a large bowl then gradually whisk in enough water to make a smooth thick icing, which coats the back of a spoon. Extra icing sugar or water can be added to reach the desired consistency.

5. Add a few drops of the food colouring and lemon extract. Spoon the icing on top of the cakes and decorate as desired. Allow the icing to set before serving.

Preparation: 30 min
Cooking time: 20 min
Serves 20

150g unsalted butter, softened
150g caster sugar
150g self-raising flour
3 eggs
1 tsp lemon extract

For the icing:
225g icing sugar, sifted
2–3 tbsp hot water
few drops yellow food colouring
½ tsp lemon extract
edible crystallised flowers, sugar
  strands, hundreds and thousands
  or sweets for decoration

Orange and poppy seed cupcakes

Preparation time: 10 min
Cooking time: 15 min
Serves 20

150g unsalted butter, softened
150g caster sugar
150g self-raising flour
2 medium eggs
grated zest ½ orange and
    1 tbsp juice
2 tbsp poppy seeds

Orange icing:
250g icing sugar
grated zest ½ orange
2–3 tbsp orange juice

To decorate:
sugared orange slices

1. Line 2 x 12-hole cupcake trays with 20 paper cases. Preheat the oven to 350°F (180°C).

2. Place the butter, sugar, flour, eggs and grated orange zest and juice in a bowl and whisk with a wooden spoon or electric whisk until pale and creamy. Stir in the poppy seeds.

3. Divide between the paper cases and level the tops. Bake for 15 minutes until golden and just firm. Cool in the tray for 5 minutes, then transfer to a cooling rack to cool completely.

4. Sift the icing sugar into a small bowl, then add the orange zest and juice. Stir until you have a smooth icing, adding a little more orange juice if necessary. Spoon over the cakes. Decorate with sugared orange slices.

White chocolate and raspberry muffins

1. Preheat the oven to 375°F (190°C). Line a muffin tray with 10 paper muffin cases.

2. In a large mixing bowl, sift the flour, baking powder and salt. Stir in the caster sugar.

3. In a jug, whisk together the egg, milk and oil with a fork. Pour over the dry ingredients and stir until just combined. Gently fold in the raspberries and chocolate chunks.

4. Spoon into the prepared cases and cook in the centre of the oven for 20–25 minutes until well risen and golden. Leave to cool in the tray for a few minutes, then transfer to a wire rack.

5. Delicious served warm or cold.

Preparation time: 10 min
Cooking time: 25 min
Serves 10

280g plain flour
1 tbsp baking powder
½ tsp salt
125g caster sugar
1 large egg, whisked
250ml milk
90ml sunflower oil
150g raspberries
150g white chocolate, roughly chopped

Pine nut muffins

1. Heat the oven to 180°C. Grease a 12-hole muffin tray.

2. Mix the flour, sugar and lemon zest in a mixing bowl.

3. Whisk the eggs into the yoghurt, then mix into the dry ingredients with the melted butter and 50g pine nuts.

4. Spoon the mixture into the tray and sprinkle the tops with the remaining pine nuts. Bake for 20–25 minutes until a skewer comes out clean.

5. Cool in the tins for 5 minutes, then place on a wire rack to cool completely.

Preparation time: 10 min
Cooking time: 35 min
Serves 12

225g self-raising flour
175g caster sugar
1 lemon, grated zest
3 eggs
7 tbsp plain yoghurt
175g butter, melted
175g pine nuts

Index

Notes

Notes

Notes

Notes

Notes

Notes

Favourite recipes

Favourite recipes

Favourite recipes

Favourite recipes

Favourite recipes